THE PHILADELPHIA
UNDERSTORY
Volume One

written & alphabetized by
Jon Spruce

Author's Disclaimer

Readers are requested to observe private property restrictions, follow the rules of the commons, pay any admission fees, and to obtain permission of landowners to view the trees, visit the sites, or to bathe in the waters mentioned in this field guide.

THE PHILADELPHIA
UNDERSTORY
Table of Contents

EPIGRAPH

All this is perfectly distinct to an observant eye
and yet could easily pass unnoticed by most.

— HD Thoreau

DEDICATION

To all my parents

AILANTHUS

When I began compiling these field guide entries into order, I really couldn't believe it at first and kept re-checking my alphabetical skills. I was convinced it had to be one of Coyote's classic pranks. From a faraway place I could hear the voice of his laughter rising to the surface of the usual city din. Suddenly it was the only thing I could hear. Ailanthus? Are you serious? How in the world does this entire field guide end up beginning with a tree like ailanthus?

In the back of my head I knew the answer wasn't anything complicated or crooked. I wrote a bunch of field guide entries, lined them up alphabetically and *ailanthus* ended up at the front of the line, position alpha in the beth. It wasn't like the alphabet was out to get me. That would be absurd, I kept telling myself, and yet it was hard to ignore the feeling that I was about to step into one of Coyote's cosmic traps.

Who else but Coyote would make sure my field guide began with the one tree that I hated the most?

I urge you to join me in this hatred. If we all hate it together, then we might actually do something about it and, people, we've got to do something. The ailanthus is already the third most common tree in the entire city, right behind the black cherry and the crabapple, and those numbers are expected to climb even higher. This is a tyrant of a tree taking over Philadelphia one open space at a time.

So keep your eyes peeled. Look for it everywhere you go in the city. I've seen it shooting out of sidewalk cracks and sprouting from potholes. It's invading the concrete islands in the middle of every highway. It could be breaking the surface of your lawn right now. I've even seen it leafing out from the sewer grates.

It usually has a thin trunk, thin enough to grasp, thin enough to strangle. It's got an offensive odor, something my dendrology professor once described as *burnt peanut butter*. It stinks the most when its leaves are crushed or its bark chipped or its trunk axed, which should be often.

When chopping one down, make sure there is nothing left behind in the ground. If any bits of root or trunk remain, it's imperative that you use the ax to slice into its still-living wood and douse the open wounds with pure alcohol, kerosene, or ultra triclopyr herbicide. Otherwise all you've done is spread this disease of a tree even more, like scratching at poison ivy.

For most people, the ailanthus is a small tree in the shape of a inconvenient wire of wood with a tropical

Ailanthus can be observed growing in different shapes and sizes throughout the city and flourishing under the most strenuous conditions.

splash of leaves growing from the top. Medium-sized ailanthus don't generally take up too much room either. As a species, their shape is extremely varied. Some grow straight and true like an oak while others display similarities to bushes and shrubs. Under the right conditions it can reach the status of a large tree and, I must admit, have an impressive presence in a landscape. The current champion ailanthus in Philadelphia is located on the corner of 13th Street and Olney Avenue in the northeast corner of an Einstein Medical Center parking lot, 58 feet tall.

Philadelphia's current champion ailanthus at 13th & Olney Streets, Einstein Medical Center; 58 ft tall, 16 ft circumpherence.

There are other contenders, if someone wants to waste the time measuring them. I think right away of the tall, husky ailanthus with black bark just a few blocks away from my West Philly urban cabin, towering over the utility wires. I found another notable one further into my neighborhood at the intersection of four tight backyards, sucking the steel posts of the fences right into its poisonous trunk.

Most people recognize the ailanthus by its leaves. They're large. They're compound, ten to twenty sharp leaflets along each petiole. On very successful ailanthus there could be as many as thirty or forty. That kind of foliage might make you think that despite the invasive nature of the tree it'd be welcome in certain parts of the city, say, along some greenless street baking under the sun. You might be fooled into thinking this tree has value, that at the very least it might provide good shade for the hard-working pedestrians of the neighborhood. I see your point. In the land of all-sun, even the shade from an ailanthus could be an oasis but it's an unpleasant kind of shade. It's fuzzy, foggy, and itchy and after a couple minutes my throat will start to close up, like I've been caught chewing hair.

It goes by other names. Its original name translated to *tree reaching for the sky*, which was later shortened to *tree of heaven*. That name is a joke. It's native to China where it's called *chouchun*, which translates to *foul smelling tree*. That name is a little better. Because of the tropical look of its foliage it's sometimes called *ghetto palm* but I don't like using that term. That makes it sound like the tree is only a problem for the more impoverished parts of the city. This is everybody's problem. The ailanthus does not discriminate between the rich or poor, or the safe or dangerous neighborhoods. It's everywhere, from Society Hill to West Oak Lane, all over South Philly, and all the way down the Roosevelt Boulevard.

And it doesn't stop at our city borders. The ailanthus can be found throughout the entire megalopolis and beyond: down in Florida, up in Massachusetts, yonder in Texas, and as west as Washington State. It's already been spotted climbing up the Rockies and circling the southwestern Turtle Island deserts, coast to coast continental domination in its grasp.

No one is innocent when it comes to the history of its proliferation and all fingers rightly point to Philadelphia. It begins in 1784 with William Hamilton, a nurseryman operating out of West Philly, not too far from my own urban cabin. He transports the ailanthus from England, a new tree in his usual shipment. Thanks to the public's burgeoning interest in Asian landscaping, he has reasonable hopes that the ailanthus will be a fine seller.

The next culprit? Andrew Jackson Downing, fifty years later, who writes a review of the plant in his best-selling horticulture magazine. He calls it *a picturesque tree* and a fast grower. He notes that it seems impervious to the insects humiliating our own native species.

Soon the ailanthus becomes one of the most common trees planted inside Philly parks and courtyards and along the streets and paved paths. Other cities follow suit, the fools. At some point, the horticulturalists realize their mistake and start publishing condemnations but the cities still buy up the nursery stocks to decorate their grids. Warnings come from all over the plant world but the damage was done, the enemy already inside the gate.

Eventually the public joins the backlash and begins protesting against its spread. This is when things get nasty and irrational. The plant becomes the subject of countless complaints and a scapegoat for a score of illnesses: sore throats, upset stomachs, *vertigo and vomiting* according to a letter in the Times, general malaise, even tuberculosis. The criticism takes on racist overtones when people start comparing its success to the influx of Chinese immigrants. Even its original champion begins calling it a *usurper* and, in one of the biggest turnarounds in botanical history, only ten years after his original rave, Andrew Jackson Downing writes in his same magazine: *down with ailanthus!*

It was ten years too late.

This will be hard to believe but the ailanthus is currently enjoying a small comeback campaign. It seems to be coming from a group of professors in the field of spontaneous urban ecology. They're asking us to put aside our hatred and to appreciate the ailanthus for what it is: one of the most successful plants to ever

Andrew Jackson Downing (1815 - 1852);
died at age 36 when the steamer ship the Henry Clay caught fire;
editor of The Horticulturalist magazine;
"Plant spacious parks in your city..."

survive the urban jungle. They say the ailanthus is sometimes the only exhibit of nature to thrive in certain parts of the city, where even the downtrodden and the underserved can look up to the ailanthus and hope that, one day, they too can succeed on these mean streets.

Hogwash.

I'll give this weed tree a few points for its tenacity but that's all it gets. That's all it deserves.

Although, to be honest, as much as I despise the plant, I have to admit: I do like that it has something to say. Sometimes I even sing the same song. You cannot stop the wilds. You can steal it from the Indians and pave it over with cement, plan out the grid, number the streets, scoop out the subway, stack the buildings and stack the people but even a city is permeable when it comes to the wilds.

We still live among the wilds: ailanthus in the gutter, deer on the shoulder, virus on the trolley, mold in the basement, rats in the sewer, seagulls of the dumpsters, cockroaches in the kitchen sink. One time I saw a frog in Whole Foods hiding in the asparagus. One time in Queen's Village I had a squirrel living in the walls of my apartment that used to keep me up all night long. For some reason I waited three days before telling the landlord. There is a germinating force in this city that cannot be stopped, will never be tamed. There's chaos lurking around every corner, at the top of every staircase, bugs in every sidewalk crack, seeds in every door jamb. All it needs is a little time and space to call its own so it can go wild once again.

I hope the same can be said about you.

ALDER

It's a spring tree for me, but barely spring, the very beginning of the Budding Trees Moon, the middle of mean March. It'll still be cold and windy and I'll be impatient for some token of spring, longing for a flower and hungry for fresh fruit. Perfect time to go alder hunting.

That's when it flowers, these long, pendant catkins dangling next to last year's cones, still hanging on, both spring and autumn on the same twig. The catkins start off brown and tight. Then they fluff out a little bit revealing shades of green and purple. I'll admit, it's not what the poets have in mind when they gush about spring flowers but at that time of year I'm not picky.

The alder belongs to the birch family and like all members of that family it has an unquenchable thirst for water. So if you find one, then you must be in sight of, or in the audience of, some Philadelphia ripple. There are some impressive ones inside the swamps of Tinicum. I've also found them growing on the beaches of the Schuylkill River and living in the big puddle near the entrance to Morris Arboretum. I've never seen any growing along the Wissahickon but I'm assuming it happens.

One time, I found a small group of alders at a place called Ten Mile Point, northeast of Center City, from the Cottman Avenue exit off 95 and up State Road where the Pennypack Creek flows into the Delaware River. This is a section of the city notorious for its number of prisons, reformatories, and juvie halls. This must be correction country. Every fortress is a different level of security but everybody is welcome to the park that lies along the shore. Pennypack on the Delaware is what it's called. It's big and beautiful but don't go there expecting a lot of adventure. Go for the chance of a long, flat promenade. Go to sit in a gazebo to watch the great Delaware River roll on by, the continent's longest undammed free-flowing river this side of the Mississippi. There's also baseball diamonds and soccer fields if you're into that kind of thing. The best part of the park is discovered along its southern boundary: an old stone wall, about seven feet tall and two feet thick, falling apart in the best way. I

am guessing that it's a relic from an industry that long forsook these Delawarian shores. It's fun to imagine it was once part of an older, stonier version of the current prison complex.

I followed the stone wall to the riverbank and walked through stands of sumac and honey locust, all trees still bare and leafless. This was early April after a record-breaking winter. There was a hazy sheen everywhere I looked, a constant breeze everywhere I turned, and a metallic taste to the air overall. The only color? Daffodils in the brown grass. When I finally made it to the riverbank, I found it covered in rubble. Some of the junk I could recognize: a park bench, a chunk of street, a manhole cover, rods of corrugated galvanized steel. It felt like I was strolling through the wreckage of a once great city, washed ashore. I found a bunch of willows growing in a tight hedge, sycamores tearing apart the woodwork of an abandoned pier, and situated closer to

the river that group of alders reaching toward the Delaware River, full of flowers and cones.

The cones, when they finally drop, are a significant source of food for grazing, herbivorous fish, for bottom feeders like catfish and eel, and for shrimp.

The alder tree doesn't have a significant population here in the Philadelphia understory. It's not used as a street tree. I've never seen it planted in a garden or campus. There are no alders on Alder Street. So if you find one or a group of them, then it's time to take a break and make a report of your surroundings. You're probably on your own, off the grid. Maybe you made a successful escape for the day and got away from it all, and now you find yourself somewhere close to old, slow, free flowing water.

The Delaware River is the 3rd greatest river on the eastern seaboard, per Prof. Dunkelmeyer's rankings; the Delaware is the eastern border of Philadelphia.

Alder trees in bloom in the big puddle near the entrance to Morris Arboretum.

ALMOND STREET

North of Center City, the Bridesburg neighborhood is a crowded part of town that was built up by its bootstraps. Its people are devoted to the place, almost to a fault, and are known throughout the rest of Philly for being industrious, close-knit, forthright, and proud of hard work. The entire neighborhood stretches along the Delaware in the shadow of two big bridges – the Betsy Ross and the Tacony Palmyra – and it's bisected by Interstate-95. For most people, Bridesburg is just a quick blur along the highway: rooftops, billboards, steeples, water towers. Even if you need to enter the actual neighborhood, it's usually in and out.

Almond Street looks like any other street in Bridesburg. In a blind taste test, it'd be hard to tell it apart from, say, Belgrade or Thompson, two streets running parallel to Almond. It's about five miles long all together. Like most small streets here in the city, it disappears every now and then as it runs through the grid, making room for some train tracks and a Home Depot, only to reappear a few blocks later. When it finally does end, Almond comes crashing to a stop right at Bridge Street, never to return.

Underneath the bridge at Bridge and Almond, there is a small creek.

That's the part that fascinates me.

There used to be a federal arsenal here at the end of Almond. It lasted from 1818 to 1977, from James Madison to Jimmy Carter. You don't hear about it too much anymore – the entire operation has been repurposed into a charter school, a business park and warehouses – but it used to be a huge part of the neighborhood, thousands of workers strong. It was like a fort in a big city with its own police force and fire department. For over 150 years, it was a productive employee for the military-industrial complex, manufacturing everything from gunpowder to LASER-guided ballistic missiles.

But Bridesburg is also river and forest country. Look at some old maps and the names of the enterprises roll off the tongue: Smedley Brothers Lumber & Mill, Fishman's Wool Pulling Factory, Loyerings Barrel. On the oldest street map I could find, less than a mile away from the arsenal, in the blue paint of the Delaware River, there are three words: *Point No Point*. That's what Bridesburg used to be called. On the same old map, right at the intersection of future-day Almond & Bridge, there is only one word: *Ferry*.

It's hard to imagine needing a ferry to cross the water that currently sits underneath the Bridge at Almond. This is a small creek, lapping its way through the backyards. Looking over the railings I could see right to the bottom of the channel, to its jagged floor of rocks, cinder blocks, sneakers, and soda cans. In some spots, it didn't look deep enough for a paper boat.

My first time there I went searching for its source, a journey that took me back down Almond, around the corner to Belgrade, only to be blocked by the impenetrable fences of a chemical plant.

Later that evening, I continued the search online and hovered the satellite over the Bridesburg map. The chemical plant was huge, much bigger than it looked from ground level. It looked like its own mini-metropolis but one made by the machines themselves, a sprawling landscape of industrial fans, cranes, cooling towers, stovepipes and smokestacks. I felt like I'd seen this kind of place before, that actually I've been seeing this kind of heavy machinery my whole life but this was the first time I ever seriously thought about how a place like this worked or what it produced.

Evidently this one was a creek factory. When I zoomed in closer, I could see the creek beginning its course from inside the fenced-in area, appearing out of the ground like any other piece of the Mechadelphia infrastructure. It burst into life in between a bunch of phenol tanks.

According to some people, one day we'll be manufactured in the same way.

Even more mysterious: this creek had no name. Earlier in the day, when I was street level, I just assumed it was the Frankford because I always thought of Bridesburg as part of the Frankford Creek watershed but, when I started dragging the satellite around the chemical plant and through the neighborhood, I saw my mistake and realized that this little creek wasn't the Frankford at all. The Frankford was actually a mile south running straight through the Port Richmond neighborhood and flowing into the Delaware River at the Betsy Ross delta.

The Frankford may not get as much acclaim as the bigger creeks in town, like the Wissahickon or the Pennypack, but it was once the hardest working creek in the entire city. So hard working that, by the 1930s, the water was completely polluted. According to one letter to the editor: *purple and perfumed*. If you ever meet an oldtimer from either Bridesburg or Port Richmond, ask them about it. I've met a few who can still remember certain summer days when the smell of the Frankford stunk up the entire neighborhood.

On old maps you can still see the creek's original course through both Port Richmond and Bridesburg. That route through both neighborhoods was one of its biggest bends, a long slow horseshoe that detoured all the ships through the factories and forests of Bridesburg. It was a passage notorious for its inconvenience, so, in an effort to speed up production and maximize efficiency, the Citymakers decided to correct the course. They bent that part of the Frankford straight, the maniacs. Now it runs as a direct line to the Delaware River through Port Richmond, never reaching the shores of Bridesburg again.

But the joke's on them. Coyote strikes again. There's still a tiny piece of that original Frankford left behind in Bridesburg: the short dogleg of a creek I found on that afternoon. It's still flowing under Bridge, stamped into the grid like any other street running parallel to Almond.

Shift is Proposed in the Course of Frankford Creek

$4,720,000 Program Would Change Face of Much of Bridesburg

By JOHN C. CALPIN
Of The Bulletin Staff

A major face-lifting of a large part of Bridesburg, including a change in the course of Frankford Creek as a flood control measure, was suggested yesterday to Mayor Samuel.

IF COURSE OF FRANKFORD CREEK IS CHANGED

Proposed channel would parallel Pennsylvania Railroad-Seashore Line tracks to point two miles south of present confluence. Upstream, new bulkheads would be built

From top to bottom: article from the Philadelphia Bulletin, 2/1/1948; satellite photo of the Almond & Bridge Streets intersection; view from standing on Bridge looking west.

With no name.

I love its anonymous nature but it's hard to believe it can go much longer without a name. How long can anything in this city go without being named or tagged or ticketed? I can see it now: some bored but earnest comptroller, slaving away in the Municipal Building office, finally noticing, by happenstance, that this little creek has been left behind. He's a real roger-dodger so he makes a big deal about it. Emails are sent with great urgency. One meeting leads to more meetings until a committee is formed. A vote is taken, a decision is made, and before you can even speak on its behalf the citymakers add another name to the already cluttered map.

According to some people, one day we'll receive our own names through the same kind of process.

For a couple of years, I taught nutrition lessons to the kids who attended the afterschool programs at the Bridesburg rec centers. I was assigned two lessons per month at the rec center right on Almond just a few blocks from where it ends at Bridge Street. The job didn't last long. The last time I was there, the kids were a nightmare but I couldn't blame them. It was one of those spectacular May afternoons and because of me they were cooped up inside the center learning about hummus instead of running around the building, screaming in the playground, or climbing over the fences.

After the lesson, I walked down to Bridge Street to visit the anonymous crick, a habit I'd gotten into every time I finished my lessons on Almond. Whenever I think about it, I always picture the creek the way it was that last time I was there, not that there was anything different or peculiar about the water that day. It was just like all the other times I went in and out of Bridesburg. There were clouds on its surface, beautiful clouds swimming in place, and black willows on top of the banks bending over their reflections. The sign at Rose Funeral Home said the same thing it always said: *additional parking in the back*. The traffic was zooming by me, so fast it seemed to make the whole creek ripple. There were ducks. There will always be ducks and, for the time being, there was Honeywell Resins & Chemicals in the background, working hard.

AMELANCHIER

A little tree with a little berry, both with too many names.

To the north, on the Canadian side of the Great Lakes and throughout the St. Lawrence River valley, the berry is called *saskatoon*, a corruption of a Cree nation word that translated to "fruit from the tree with many branches." The Saskatchewan province shares the same corrupted root word and roughly translates to "place where saskatoons grow abundantly." Saskatchewan's largest city is the same name as what they call the fruit, Saskatoon. On Saskatoon's flag is a rendering of the tree's typical twig with small oval leaves and purple olive-shaped fruit. It's great to see a flag being used as a field guide.

Native only to Turtle Island, the saskatoon is one of the first edible tree-fruits of the growing season. Along with *saskatoon*, it's also called the *sugarplum* or the *chuckleberry*. According to Thoreau, in Cape Cod they call it the *joshpear*. I think most people south of Saskatoon probably know it as the *juneberry*, for obvious reasons but I'll say it anyway. It ripens in June, between strawberries and blueberries. It's never had a prominent place in the market or the kitchen but it's a favorite for Indians and foragers whose recipes call for baking them in a pie or pudding or drying them for cereal and pemmican. They're delicious, a combination of dark cherry and plum with a hint of maple syrup.

Keep your eyes open for the juneberry in the upcoming years. It's on Big Ag's fast track for mass production but even the smaller family farms are interested. I know one farmer out near Gettysburg who's planted three rows of the tree and expects to bring them to the Philadelphia farmers' markets within the next five years, cannot wait.

My prediction? This berry will soon become another hero in the superfruit pantheon. Most likely they'll be marketed in the same manner that catapulted cranberries to stardom: canned concentrates, flavored ice teas, probiotic cleanses, and gourmet trail mixes. I wonder which name will get Big Ag's approval. I'm rooting for saskatoon.

In the forest, it's notable for being one of the first trees to flower, a bright white bloom in an otherwise bare and silvery wood. In the last few years I've noticed different varieties of them used as street trees, beautiful but mutant ornamental cousins to the hardy forest folk. In the street tree catalogs, there are several different

hybrids to choose from: *coles select, regent saskatoon, shadblow,* the *Allegheny,* to name a few. They're planted primarily for the splendor of their blossoms and yet those blossoms tend to get lost, dwarfed, and overshadowed by the bigger blooms of the season like the pear, the magnolia, and the cherry.

They deserve a better look. The flowers grow in a loose, very pleasing pattern called a *simple raceme,* where each flower in the bunch grows at the end of a thin stalk and each stalk is an equal distance apart. Like most flowers in the Rose family, they have five petals. These five are bright white and look like they're being flung off the branches. When the wind blows through them they spin around like propellers.

In most field guides, their bloom is described as *a seasonal clock* because it used to serve as a signal, or an alarm, for the people living a more agrarian, less electronic way of life. I don't like that I'm about to follow in this field guide tradition — I wouldn't wish being a clock on my own worst enemy – but I do like how each time the flowers strike, depending where and whom you are, a different tale is told.

At the end of each tale the tree usually gets a new name.

One of the more interesting of those names has to do with funeral services. This would take place somewhere along the frontier, say, on a farm on the outskirts of a little wooden town. The season? It's that glorious, noisy switch from winter into spring. According to the few Indians that still hang around the wooden town, this time of year is called the Budding Trees Moon, first moon of Wabun the Golden Eagle, spirit keeper of the East, dandelion by day, frogsong at night.

I spend the cold mornings trying to light a fire in the Franklin stove, fill up the coffee pail with well water, feed the cats and ducks, and collect the eggs from all the coops. Then I go about making breakfast and pasta dough while my wife milks the goats and starts making the cheese. Later that afternoon, when running the alpacas along the creek, I see the tree in flower and, like I would with any good clock, I'll know it's time for certain tasks and responsibilities, for seasonal rites and ceremonies. I'll know it's time to bury the dead. The flowers tell me the land is thawed enough to dig the graves. Growing up in these parts, you go to funeral services with this tree in bloom. That's why I know the tree as the *serviceberry*. Other people round here here know it as the *servicetree* and the real rural folk call it the *sarvisberry*.

I'll also know it's time to plant the garden, hopefully with the sprouts we've been tending to indoors since the vernal equinox. The two services mirror each other at this time of year. The seed is buried, the soul is planted. Heading back home, I'll also remember that, once word gets to town that the serviceberry is flowering, the preacherman usually starts his way down the country roads. He's leaving town to assist with those burials, to lead the services, and to go from cabin to cabin to hand out Bibles and convert the frontier. When I tell my wife I've seen the serviceberry in bloom, she reminds me to keep the front gate locked.

If I were a colonial fisherman, then I would know the tree as the *shadbush*, or the *shadtree*, or the *shadblow*, so named because its flowering coincides with the great eastern seaboard shad migration. Shad spend their winters down south in the warm waters of the Chesapeake Bay and, every year when the shadtree blows, they swim north through the mighty river systems of the megalopolis, the Delaware, Susquehanna, Potomac, Hudson, and Connecticut. Their final destination is the Bay of Fundy, their summer haunt. The whole journey is called the *shad run* and for many generations the Philadelphia riverbanks were a bonanza of shad.

Shad Fishing at Gloucester on the Delaware River
Thomas Eakins (1881)

They are so plentiful, William Penn wrote in 1686, *that Captain Smyth's Overseer at the Skulkil drew 600 and odd at one Draught, 300 is no wonder, 100 familiarly.*

Philadelphia's own Thomas Eakins captured this riverbank scene in two paintings, both currently hanging in the American Collection at the Art Museum, first floor.

Six miles upriver from those paintings is my favorite group of shadbushes in the entire city. They're located along the Schuylkill River Trail, right below Umbria Street on the Manayunk towpath. They lean up against a stonewall, tall enough to be seen from the road when driving by. Each planting is a loose cluster of curling trunks, undoubtedly still recognizable by any Cree as the "tree with many branches."

On old maps, this part of the Schuylkill was called the Gully Run. It's also labeled Manayunk Canal Lock 68 and about a mile upriver from here by Flat Rock Dam there lies the ruins of the old lock-tender's house. His name was Captain, or sometimes *Cap'n*, Winfield Scott Guiles and he is legendary for being the lock-tender for this part of the canal for over 60 years, finally retiring in 1934. His wife was Lenape. I've found only two references to her and they both use the same name: *Manayunk Healer*. She was known around town for treating illnesses with local herbs, roots, barks, and flowers. Will somebody please write an urban fairytale about this couple? I'll even get it started for you: *a captain and a medicine woman once lived, as husband and wife, in a lock-tender's house right next to Flat Rock Dam on the Manayunk Canal. One evening right before supper there was an unexpected knock on the door that sounded like a call for help.*

"*Third time this week,*" *the Cap'n said.*

It was just spring and the shadbushes were in bloom...

Never Sleeps in Bed

WINFIELD S. GUILES

Veteran locktender at Flat Rock dam, Schuylkill River, whose sixty-ninth birthday yesterday
marked the close of 31 years during which he
has never slept in a bed, but has obtained rest
at irregular intervals while seated in a chair.

Caption reads: "Winfield S. Guiles, Veteran locktender at Flat Rock dam, Schuylkill River, whose sixty-ninth birthday yesterday marked the close of 31 years during which he has never slept in a bed, but has obtained rest at irregular intervals while seated in a chair." [source of photo unknown, found on www.findagrave.com]

Andorra Shopping Center

Spanish for *shrub-covered land*, the Andorra Shopping Center is located at the westward terminus of Henry Avenue, right on the border of Philadelphia and Montgomery counties.

I go there often. It's just down the street from the Schuylkill Center, which is my favorite woods in the entire city and the site of my friend Gina's small organic farm. The Andorra Shopping Center is a reliable place to pick up some supplies for another great hike and a good place for a quick, easy lunch. Gina is a big fan of the veggie burritos at the Machismo Burrito Bar. When they went out of business, we got addicted to the spring rolls at Ping Pong Chinese.

But it's not just the woods or the food or Gina that brings me to Andorra so often. I've gotten into the habit of visiting the shopping center whenever I feel off-kilter or out-of-whack. I go there to be soothed from those spells. I have found within its boundaries a sense of balance and concord that I cannot find elsewhere in the city. Andorra has a way of bending me back to my old used-to-be. Time there is a reset and although I may drive into its lot feeling like I'm just another robot on the assembly line, or just another alien in the solar system, or just another beast in a cage, I tend to leave the square feeling at peace, centered, and right on. For that I am grateful.

The key to the harmony becomes self-evident if you park right in its center and behold: every shop here has its own opposite, or its own complement, its own twin.

There's a Radio Shack next to a Game Stop. There's a Kohl's department store and a Dollar Express. There's a branch of the library but there's also a Bargain Book Warehouse. There are post office mailboxes right in front of a Parcel Plus. There's a Petco, a place that will groom your domesticated animals, next to a Hair Cuttery franchise. The optometrist is down the sidewalk from the Famous Footwear. There's an Extra Care doctor's office across the parking lot in case you're in need of a different kind of repair shop. The Jenny Craig store is twice as big as the GNC. The Staples store seems to be on its own, maybe the biggest sign in the entire square, but I have the funny feeling that it has some lost connection to the Modern Vacuum & Sew store, whose sign is out front every day asking the same question: *Dirty Carpets?* The T-Mobile and the iGenius seem to stare at each other from a forty-five degree angle. What is going on behind the curtains of the Serene Blü Massage & Spa? It always smells like lavender when I walk by its dark doors. Meanwhile, Best Nails has her windows wide open and always looks busy, welcoming the walk-ins. There's a dojo here called AmeriKicks and, just down the sidewalk, there's something called Mathnasium, the classic battle still raging strong: brains versus brawn, jocks versus nerds.

For food, I have almost the entire globe: Italian, Chinese, Thai, Mexican, a McDonald's and a Saladworks, plus a frozen yogurt joint and an Acme grocery store. You can burn it all off at the L.A. Fitness in the corner. There's an Applebee's, which advertises itself coast to coast as a *Neighborhood Bar & Grill.* I'm judgmental and sarcastic when it comes to these kinds of franchises but really I'm just bored. My buddy Goldberg says I should lighten up. Applebee's means well, he says. They only want to please me. All that research and development they put into that boring menu, they're really just placating my need for familiarity and rhythm, my fear of risk, my anxiety over the unknown. Nothing untested, nothing too sour or too crabby will ever slip by them, not on Applebee's watch, and yet they can still satisfy that very human itch to try something new, something adventurous, like pineapple on a pizza.

This is the niche of the trading post, the epitome of the kind of mercantile center that keeps appearing every time human beings gather, make families, build homes, develop transportation, and take root. The trees build their woods. We build our markets. It's a tradition as old as civilization, although the older and wiser cultures might be a little befuddled by our addition of the No Loitering sign. That policy is going to be hard to explain if we ever were visited by a time-traveling group of ancient customers although it does explain the lack of benches.

The threat of a fine might confuse them too. That implies the presence of an enforcer but wouldn't that be a strange sight to see: somebody going around the square issuing tickets and fines for loitering? If that's you, better bring lots of tickets. And prepare yourself for a chase. For the loiterers are cunning and hard to catch. We have the tendency to spread out over vast distances, with the uncanny ability to immediately stop our loiter and blend right back into the consuming crowd at the first sign of anything resembling an authority figure. And be prepared to defend yourself. I imagine even the smallest percentage of citizens caught in the act of loitering will fight your ticket and jam up the courts every day. After all, Your Honor, who among us Andorrians is not guilty of loitering?

I tend to pick a parking spot a safe distance from anything that looks like a group which is not always an easy thing to do. The Water Department vans and PECO trucks always seem to gather in herds. It's hard to predict where they'll set up on any given day. The police and the EMTs are never gone for long but that might have something to do with the Police & Fire Credit Union Bank tucked away in the northeast corner. I think it looks suspicious if you keep cruising up and down the lot but I see other vehicles do it without any trouble or consequence. I usually make one giant loop around the whole square before I choose my nest. I'm looking for a spot that won't make me look like a loner but I definitely want to make it obvious: I come here for the seclusion and the solitude. But the joke's on me. Coyote wins again. No matter which spot I choose, no matter how much I think I'm alone, I'm never far enough away from another shadow in another car, loiterers as far as the eye can see. We all end up in Andorra at some point. We graze in the cars. We sit in the center where the secret to the loitering policy becomes all too clear: they want us to loiter. They prefer us in idle. They like when we sit in their lines and park in their spots and they know exactly how to make us obey. They tell us it's forbidden. The enforcer is finally unmasked. He is us. And now the truth behind the policy is finally revealed: here in Andorra, it's not actually loitering that's forbidden but its opposite.

For further proof of this place's harmonious properties, I point you in the direction of the Planet Petco logo painted on the big window of the store. It depicts, in silhouette, the entire domesticated animal kingdom: dog, cat, hamster, goldfish, parakeet, gecko, guinea pig, rabbit, turtle, gerbil, ferret, lizard, parrot, the whole hysterical, goofy menagerie. They're all floating in free fall inside the circle of the logo, inside the globe. And what's in the center? By the wings of Wabun, it's tree.

This is no logo. This is a modern day petroglyph, a 21st Century cave painting. I try my best to bring this Planet Petco with me wherever I go. I carry it like a burden but I wear it like a badge. I find its message humbling and inspirational and, even though humans aren't included in the happy zoo, I think of those animals as my brothers and sisters, my roommates in the house of tree. In my most solemn moments, when I'm most in tune with the wind-water dance, I can even remember when this logo took place, way back when, long before the Great Domestication, when we all lived here on Turtle Island in harmony and equilibrium.

Apricot

While the rest of the city waits anxiously for the fickle cherry to flower, I've already watched spring bloom into season, thanks to the apricot.

This is one of our most reliable first-to-flowers, always right on time, about a dozen days past the vernal equinox, first week of cruel April, blooming on cue no matter how cold and long the winter. This is the tree that should be the star of our blossom festivals, not the cherry. The cherry is consistently tardy when it comes to flowering and just when you think it's finally showing up for the season it tends to delay even more, wishy-washy. I'd say, on average, the cherry puts on a good show maybe one out of every five years. We'd be better off casting its cousin, the apricot.

Take a look at winter 2013-14. A winter of record. Twenty-two days below freezing. Snowstorms coming in at a rapid fire click. Only one week all season long without snow on the ground. By mid-February, it was already the third snowiest winter in Philly history. The final storm on March 7th brought the total to 63 inches. Strawberries were pushed till past Memorial Day, according to one farming family, something that hadn't happened in thirty years.

And yet there was the apricot, the first week of April, full blow.

Coming to us originally from the Persian forests, the Philadelphia apricot is not the orchard tree that grows the apricot fruit but an ornamental variety bred for its flowers. It's got some plum in its genes, another one of its cousins from the Rose family. Perhaps that's why there's a little purple in the flower? Or is it pink? It's hard to tell. It's hard to focus. The light dances off these petals, pure dazzle. The flowers are numerous, close to the branch, papery, tightly wound, and small, so small that I have to walk, enchanted, under its boughs and into the tree itself to catch its details or snap a photo. I feel like a bee. From every center: a filament of pistils, every pistil topped with a single yellow bead.

I've found only three apricots in the entire city: two in Morris Arboretum and one more just seven blocks away from my urban cabin, on the way to the liquor store and the food co-op. Are there more in the city? If so, I have only one week out of the year to find them. After its bloom, I'm in the bad habit of ignoring the tree but, in all fairness, it doesn't do much for the rest of the year. Except for that one brief week in very early spring, it's just another street tree on the way to grab cheap vodka and fair-trade coffee, a humble disguise for such a stalwart herald of spring, for such a star.

The emeral ash borer, pictured here courtesy of the PA Dept. of Conservation & Natural Resources, is a very success- ful killing machine, with a 99% mortality rate against ash trees.

Ash

Citybillies, it's time to bid your farewell to the ash tree. Sorry to say that for the last dozen years the ash population on Turtle Island has been losing the battle against a swarm of emerald ash borers, a sparkly green bug less than one inch long, accidentally brought over from Asia on a pallet to Michigan. The swarm entered Pennsylvania in 2007 with over 50 million dead ashes already in its wake.

From an article in the Inquirer at the time: *"This is pretty much going to hammer ash trees in Southeastern Pennsylvania almost into oblivion,"* said Scott Guiser, an educator at Pennsylvania State University's extension service in Bucks County.

By 2021, the number of ash deaths worldwide reached 100 million.

Don't think this bug has gone unnoticed. Big Business has its hands all over the Pennsylvania ash, lots of money at stake. With a straight mast for a trunk, this is a tree made for timber, a great grower with a quick spurt. It can reach twenty-five feet in the first eight years. Even more remarkable, a stand of ash seems to grow in synchronicity, each tree in the row growing at the same rate reaching the same height year after year. This has been observed in the forests, in the tree farms, and in the ash trees planted along the same city street.

It is the premier wood when it comes to sporting equipment and tool handles, as well as the bodies and necks of electric guitars and the shells of the conga drum, plus rifle stocks and canoe paddles. It also makes excellent firewood, which is how the bug crossed so many state lines since arriving in Michigan.

In response to the bug, all states with an ash population, basically Maine to Florida and then west to Minnesota, have quarantined their firewood to their own political borders. That's a wise policy even during peacetime. Always find your fuel at the site of your fire. Do not cross firewood with state lines. One summer I was a volunteer park ranger way up in Vermont near the Canadian border, a long story, and we were trained to ask every guest as they were checking in for the night: *any firewood on you?* We also hung signs along the highway that read What Does the Ash Tree Mean to You?

For many people, the ash means baseball and this is actually a proper occasion for some good old fashioned Pennsylvania pride. Since the 1880s, Louisville Slugger's most popular choice for wood was the ash crop growing along our northernmost border. It is a known fact in the world of baseball: Pennsylvania ash is the best wood for a baseball bat, has the perfect balance of strength and resiliency, and is the only way to really make that home run thwack. Now that the bug is here, they've been making their bats more with maple but the results speak for themselves. Maplewood bats are three times more likely to break than bats made of ash. In 2010, MLB enforced a ban on ultra-light maple wood and a complete prohibition against the use of red and silver maple.

The next time you go to a Phillies game, go with ash on your mind and approach the stadium by turning east at the intersection of Broad and Pattison. They really did their homework here. For just about the entire distance from the train station to the ballpark you will be walking next to a double-row of ash trees. It's a meaningful gesture, a way to honor the ash's contribution to the game, and yet these Pattison Avenue ashes aren't faring so well. It's not the bug's fault, not this time, not that I think. Most likely they weren't given enough room. They look stressed and trapped under the full blaze of the sun. They make a sad monument actually. Some of them are completely leafless, not a scratch of green. The others have but a tuft of leaves, usually around its midsection, and no sign of life on its upper limbs.

Were they really planted as a tribute to the history of the baseball bat? I have no idea but one thing is sure. They've now become an omen for this tree's imminent demise.

From the same article in the Inquirer: *Carl Schulze, director of the division of plant industry in the N.J. Department of Agriculture, figured it was inevitable. "We're sort of resigned to the march of this."*

Catch them while you can. If you want to see what they're really like, then find them elsewhere on another street. They're used often. I have one right outside my urban cabin and it's still doing great. Or go see them in a park. There's an ash right on top of Lemon Hill in Fairmount Park standing next to a mansion but it's a mansion itself. Every time I drive nearby, it seems to beckon me to its spot on top of the hill. Every time I get close, it seems to appear out of nowhere. Or find them in the Philly woods. They're common, still in good health, tall and hefty enough to command its own space in the crowded woods. Look for their leaves. They're dark green, with super sharp points like the tips of spears ready to poke your eyes out. When the wind blows through them, it makes a terrific rustle. It roars. In the fall, it's one of the first trees to color the canopy. They burst into bright candles just when the weather turns in October, yellow and incandescent under the Ducks Fly Moon. Its bark is fascinating, a tight diamond pattern

A healthy ash bursting with foliage at 46th & Springfield, what may be a rare sight for future generations.

46

with furrows so deep that, in the dead of winter, they're often packed with snow.

Is there anything we can do to protect it from extinction? Is there any way to stop the bug? There are measures being taken. In some parts of Pennsylvania, the foresters are creating firewalls between infected and healthy populations, actually cutting down swaths of healthy trees to keep the bug at bay. In other corners of the hot zone, it's biological warfare. They're introducing from Asia its natural predators, two species of parasitic wasps. I don't know. I got a bad feeling about this. It's a military strategy borrowed from the Godzilla movies. We got to let loose a bigger monster to protect us from the other monster spoiling our game, stealing our business, marching to our city, and eating through our forests. The ending to this battle has yet to be writ and there's still hope for the ash's survival, so why do I have a sinking feeling that I've seen this movie before?

Bartram Oak, *Quercus x heterophylla*

Bartram's Garden

Founded in 1728, Bartram's is Amercia's oldest surviving botanical garden and the site of some of Philadelphia's oldest trees. It's tucked away behind an apartment complex at 54th Street and Lindbergh Boulevard, right along the crookedest part of the Schuylkill River. It's a common practice to remark that this location is smack-dab in a neighborhood that's seen better days.

I wonder if that's really true. I wonder if this neighborhood, which was named Chinsessing by the Lenape, "place where there is a meadow," later changed to Kingsessing, ever had the kind of good old days that we associate with Olde City, or Germantown, or even Kensington.

I went online to look at some old maps. Maybe I could find those better days.

On a map from 1808, the Bartram Botanical Garden is right where it should be. There really isn't anything else around it. This part of Philadelphia was its oldest settlement but it doesn't look very settled. The closest neighbor is a fishery to the south. I see two creeks nearby: the Perch and the Mill. Off to the west, there's something called Sorrel Horse Tavern & School, two institutions you don't often see sharing the same house.

On the next map from 1862, the grid really comes to life with a checkerboard of streets. Most of them are numbered, still numbered to this day. A railroad runs right through what's now called Old Botanic Garden. This part of the Schuylkill River is illustrated with clumps of reeds and labeled *marsh*. The two creeks have survived but the Tavern & School is now called Sorrel Horse Inn.

The next map is from 1895. Mill Creek is gone but the Perch still runs. I can't find anything labeled Sorrel Horse. I'm afraid it might've turned into something called the Belmont Cricket Club. The railroad is now called Philadelphia-Reading and the whole neighborhood has really exploded into detail. I see lots of plant nurseries and some schools, although the area by the river is still left undeveloped. It's now called Bartram Park.

The next map from 1903 is strictly a street and rail map, although I still see Perch Creek and I still see Bartram's as a green square simply labeled Park. The next map is just a few years later in the bright future of 1910. It's once again labeled Bartram Park and the Belmont Cricket Club comes back. Perch Creek still runs. It looks like the nurseries have become lumber yards and Bartram's gets its first neighbor, the Gulf Refining Company.

Next up is a 1942 land use map and the river shore is suddenly booming with business: Water Terminal Fuel Oil Company, City of Philadelphia Garbage Disposal Plant, Grays Ferry Brick Company, Seaboard Container Corporation, the Warner Company Building Materials, then Bartram Park, followed by the United State Gypsum Company and the Socony Vacuum Oil Company Incorporated. Perch Creek is gone. The apartment complex that shields Bartram's from Lindbergh Boulevard gets its first name: the United States Defense Housing Village. The Belmont Cricket Club is now the Kingsessing Playground.

And today? What's this neighborhood like today?

Brother, it ain't pretty. Lindbergh Boulevard on the way to Bartram's is a silent ride through retail long sold out, industry long gone. Rows and rows of empty warehouses. Factories orange from the rust. Construction projects in neglect. Someone has stapled signs on just about every telephone pole: *We Buy Houses.* Sometimes I see people working inside the parking lots but what are they doing? Standing in the center of the lot alone listening to their cell phones on an urgent looking call, or it's a small group of clipboard carriers wandering from corner to corner, or someone's moving a container, or someone's parking a crane. A closer look along the boulevard reveals some industries hanging on. I see signs for Crescent Iron Works and Kempf Building Supply and $$$ Scrap Metal $$$. Down 51st Street, there's a brick building labeled Dept of Streets Construction and Facilities Management. Across the street from that, in another big parking lot, there's a fleet of garbage trucks and rows and rows of Gold Medal Dumpsters. The river is blocked off everywhere with fences.

But turn down Harley Avenue, just before 54th Street, and turn back the clock to the good old days of colonial Philadelphia. Down the wooded lane, Bartram's Garden awaits.

It always takes me a good hour of sauntering to remember how best to enjoy this garden. This place doesn't reward the rushed, doesn't cater to the person pressed for time. Like a used bookstore, the proper pace is a browse, the proper gait a stroll. And also like a used bookstore I find myself reading the names on the plaques hanging from the trees like titles on the spines of books. I quietly say their names out loud as I browse up and down the wooded corridors.

Spend even more time at Bartram's and a new set of names is conjured up and spoken aloud. I'm embarrassed to admit this but surely I can't be the only one who's ever slipped into the vortex and slipped back in time here at Bartram's. It's commonplace to say there is *history* in this garden but if we could look through the eyes of its oldest trees could we use the word *memory*? There does seem to be a deep, shared memory lurking on these grounds. If I can tap into it then the names get even more prestigious, like Washington, Jefferson, Madison, Adams, Hamilton, Franklin, and that's just counting the currency.

They used to loiter here, the whole rebellious gang, escaping from downtown Independence Hall to visit their friends the Bartrams, out past the meadows of West Philly. Walking down these same paths I can imagine them clustered in the distance, silhouetted against the next rise in the hills, arguing over a turn of phrase or the price of tea. I get the feeling that, while at Bartram's, ordinary acts and boring conversations are outlawed but all I can add to the conversation is my quiet chant through the garden: honey locust, pin oak, sourwood, pignut hickory.

Some of the individual trees even take on presidential personalities. Next to the stone house, there's a southern magnolia that I swear is the spitting image of George Washington. That was one of his favorite trees. Mount Vernon has a whole

section of its garden dedicated to the magnolia. He even named his horse Magnolia.

Around the corner, there is a Virginia pine and I can't help but think of Thomas Jefferson. In his book, *Notes on the State of Virginia*, he tries to list all the native flora and fauna of his home state. It's an incredibly boring thing to read and yet each name on the list is the equivalent of staking a flag in the ground. This is our island, he seems to be saying, and these trees and plants, flowers, vines, shrubs and weeds, that's country.

And on every trip, even though it's far from the tallest tree in the garden, it's always the curious franklinia that looms largest, named for Ben Franklin. He and John Bartram were contemporaries, part of the older generation of Philadelphia troublemakers. John Bartram purchased the land that would become this garden around the same time Ben Franklin purchased his first newspaper. I feel remiss not including more biography of John Bartram or his son, William, but they lived too

much saga and scholarship to even broach the subject here. Let it be said that they were friends to the minuteman and the Indian alike, able to hobnob with both the president and the pioneer, the white pine and the joe-pye weed. Let me sum it up by saying that the Bartrams, both father and son, had some of the most important and productive adventures ever through the swamps and forests of America, and enough discoveries to make any tree-hunter blush with envy.

I guess that's why I always feel a little professional jealousy whenever I approach a franklinia, the lost camellia, one of John Bartram's greatest finds. He discovered it in the Carolina swamps while lost on an expedition, brought it up north with the rest of the specimens, and it hasn't been seen in the wilds since. He saved it from extinction, or from being lost forever. Now every known franklinia in the world shares an ancestor with the franklinia that Bartram rescued from the swamps and planted in West Philly.

You can currently find a real bushy one behind the stone house near the veggie garden. There are a few other around town, most notably one planted in my neighborhood at 42nd and Spruce Streets. The owner has put a small stone sign at its base with this handwritten note: *1763 Franklinia only one wild seed propagated by John Bartram, America's first naturalist at his garden near here. Named for his good friend Dr. Ben Franklin. This one + or - 100 yrs.* There's another one planted at Independence Hall. When planted in a historic place it becomes a monument, the tree as statue. The tallest one I've ever seen lives in the Jefferson Hospital garden, 9th and Pine. I like to visit the tree at the end of July to see its flower: a very large, bright white flower with a sunny yellow center, like an egg.

John's son William also had lots of adventures mucking through the southern swamps so there is a large population of southern trees in the garden. Except for the franklinia, I'm not that wild about that part of the selection. I find that I don't have an affinity for southern trees in general, so for me there's about ten too many magnolias and about three too many silverbells, although I read once that the silverbell was one of Washington's favorites. The ironwoods are fun to see but we have nothing to say to each other, nothing to share. I feel the same way about the sourwood.

But those are mere quibbles. The garden has lots of trees that are not to be missed. I keep a mental list of my own favorites that I check off during each visit like a roll call. This includes the ginkgo near the entrance, oldest surviving ginkgo on the continent, planted in 1785, a behemoth that's trying to rip a hole in the sky; a black walnut near the parking lot; a bur oak that I like to know is still there; the Bartram oak, a rare, naturally occuring hybrid named for the family; what's left of the yellowwood that was blowed down during the Great Gale of 2010; a catalpa with beans so long they stretch from belt to shoe; the buttonbush on the side of the house, how it always seems to flower the biggest during the Fourth of July weekend; there's an osage orange hiding in the weeds along the river-path; there are water-lilies in the reflecting pool; fig trees by the arbor; a wildflower patch with asters, echinacea, thistles and yarrow; I sometimes see wild turkeys bouncing with a panic across the lawn; I even like the view of the skyline from the parking lot.

As I'm leaving, it always occurs to me: I appreciate most what I don't see here. I've never run into a guided tour, never stepped into a tourist trap. I've never been hit up for an admission price, run into a fake grave, or bumped into some sweaty actor in a Ben Franklin bib or a Betsy Ross frock. It's just far enough away from all those downtown gift shops and it's got too many bad neighborhoods in between to find a spot on a tight tourist itinerary. With all of its history and memory, there must've been some talk of turning this garden into a theme park but, in the end, perhaps that kind of idea was deemed too ordinary for such a place as this.

Without the kind of phony props and facades that you find in Olde City and Elfreth Alley, this place isn't really toured. It's used. After all these years, that's still the most remarkable thing about it. During any stroll, no matter the season, I always see the neighborhood using the place: picnicking in the grass, harvesting vegetables from the community garden, sitting in front of a tree with a sketchbook, posing for engagement cards or senior prom photos, the kids from the apartments racing their bikes through the dandelions, building forts in the snow, the boats in the background tugging down the dirty river, or the modern renegade browsing from tree to tree, nothing better to do on this fine day but memorize more names, make new friends, on this most presidential of grounds.

Three highlights from the garden:
(above left) *franklinia flower;* (above right) *oldest ginkgo in
North America;* (below) *the flower of the buttonbush shrub.*

BASSWOOD

The basswood is part of the linden tree genus, famous for its wood. It's very common here in Philadelphia, found frequently on the streets, in the parks, down the trails and in the woods. They don't get as much attention as other giant trees like oaks and sycamores but they have the potential to be just as tall and mighty. In fact, if there are no oaks and sycamores in your neighborhood, and no spruce or tulip poplars too, then the biggest tree on your block might just be a basswood.

Its leaf is in the shape of an asymmetrical heart, its color a dark green on the upper side and a lighter shade of lime underneath. When caught in a breeze the two contrasting shades of green create a twinkling effect upon the tree. They're fully leafed out before they go into their flowering season which usually begins in June.

The flowers are small, even for a flower. They swing down like a little bell from a tiny cord that's connected to the stem and the heartleaf. They're usually creamy white, but when full of pollen a dusty yellow. Fans of the basswood gush over their honeyed scent but despite many sniffs and snuffles I've never had the pleasure. The bees disagree with me. They swarm the blooming basswood to such a degree that older field guides use them as a way to distinguish the basswood from other June flowerers.

Listen for a gentle uninterrupted buzz of bees, you might see in their linden chapter. *Most likely basswood.*

By November, the flowers have turned into hard brown nutlets, rodent food, and the leaves have turned to a pleasant, but not a blazing, shade of yellow. Usually by the end of fall, the leaves show extensive signs of consumption. Basswood foliage feeds a diverse and destructive group of insects: caterpillars, inchworms, beetles, flies, aphids, and the larvae of leaf miners. On the mammal side of things, chipmunks, mice, and porcupines are usually listed among its frequent diners. What I wouldn't give to see a porcupine eating basswood leaves. In the winter, deer and cottontails eat the twigs. I like its bark a lot, long lines of tough cork running up and down the tree. Native Americans used to make rope from the inner part of this bark, the part called the *bast*, which is why we started calling this tree the *basswood*. To make the rope, the Native Americans kept the bast submerged in lakes and ponds for months before it was ready to braid. They used the leftover fibers from the rope-making process to make sewing thread.

Its wood is soft with few grains. The Vikings used the basswood to make their shields and it's always been good material for crates, boxes, shutters, yardsticks, and picture frames. They make a good ruler. It is the most popular choice for venetian blinds, one of my favorite props in one of my favorite movie genres. It's also the wood of choice for sculpting, especially for old-fashioned toys and marionettes. The Iroquois made masks out of this tree. They cut faces into the trunk, then carefully chopped the image out of the tree and scooped the wood out from the back of the face.

For notable ones here in Philadelphia, I know of two. The first one can be found in Washington Square Park, close to the

7th and St. James intersection. A very odd looking tree, its roots are all cramped and twisted into the shape of a rectangular box, like someone was trying to stunt its height when it was younger by locking it up in a box. It spent its first years taking the shape of its jail. And then the box, or whatever it was, disappeared and the tree went back to normal and started growing its trunk straight up into the sky. Now it looks like a tree growing out of a big block of wood, which I guess is true of all trees but this basswood really drives that point home.

The other notable one lives in Dickinson Square Park in the Pennsport neighborhood, South Philly, along Moyamensing Avenue. I used to manage the Sunday morning farmers' market in that park. When I wanted to change the market's cover photo for Facebook, I'd take the shot from behind that basswood while standing on top of a nearby park bench, year after year, every three months a new photo, to show the change of season. There was a way to take the photo that made it look like the basswood was looking over us, bending over the vendors in a protective, almost fatherly way. Truth was it was trying to avoid the sycamore growing behind it.

I'm sure there are many other remarkable basswoods throughout Philly's woodlands and parklands, but those two are really the only ones that are memorable for me. I am embarrased to admit that my list of notable basswoods remains so short, embarrassed but not surprised when it comes to the basswood. This is a tree that for all its ubiquity and utilities rarely gets me buzzing. It's certainly not for lack of trying. It's everywhere, used frequently inside the grid and a repetitive feature inside the woods. I can recognize it instantly, can see it coming from a distance as I walk up the street or blaze down the trail. Its traits are interesting, and its natural history has some great tales to tell, so I keep feeling the nudge toward the direction of affection, at the very least some sort of respect, but I never get that far. I just keep going.

I get the sense the feeling is mutual despite, or perhaps on account of, my own ubiquity.

I'll put the blame on myself. I must be another kind of urban porcupine who must be looking for something else in a tree, something that is not inherent in the basswood. Or there's something not inherent in me to see what the basswood could offer, does offer, to a more deserving soul. What is it, exactly, that I'm looking for in a tree? That's not an easy question for me to answer. Let's just say I want my tree to be more than just good wood.

*The Dickinson Square Farmers' Market, located in Pennsport
neighborhood at Moyamensing Ave. and Morris St.,
open Sunday mornings, year-round.*

BEECH

Awakening one August morning, I realized that I had the whole day to myself. No promises, no obligations, no dues.

Ah, summer.

Like most people with a summer day to burn, I went down to the beach, this time to the banks of the Schuylkill River. I had my old trusty camping chair in one hand, a new paperback in the other. Unlike most beaches, this shore was never crowded, located off the river-trail in Bartram's Garden, an isolated shingle of mud hidden from the masses.

I chose a spot near the river's edge next to a small gathering of strange plants. They grew stalks instead of trunks and they were squirming out of the sand like giant heads of celery with thick rubbery leaves on top. As I sat down in my chair, those leaves formed a curtain between my perch and the rest of the busy world.

The sunshine glared off the beach, lighting up every pebble, every half-buried rock, every stray two-by-four and soda can washed ashore. I untied my sneakers and took my first deep breath of the day. The wind was blowing both jasmine and diesel, pulling the waves towards my feet on a string. Hovering above me in the distance across the river: the city skyline and its million eyes but, for the moment, I felt secluded and solitary.

Except for the dead fish staring right at me.

I don't know my fishes like I know my trees but I was pretty sure it was a carp, although I do admit I call any earthling that looks like a giant goldfish a carp. This one was stuck in the stalks of the plants, just hanging out in midair about two feet above the ground. It was buzzing with flies and bloated from the heat, tight as a drum. With its mouth and eyes wide open, the carp died with a look of both fear and astonishment frozen across its face. I've been seeing that same look all over the city lately, and not just from the Goldfish People. It was like we were all getting caught in the stalks, stuck in the weeds floating around watching the water drain to the bottom of the river and there was nothing we could do but watch.

I took another deep breath. I was determined not to let cold thoughts like that ruin my summer day here at the beach or let it stop me from sinking into the curious novel I'd discovered in the stacks of a used bookstore.

It was called *Strange Proximities* by Clarissa "Butcher" Cassady. On its cover was an astronaut in an unearthly landscape, red moons in a black sky. A green plant enveloped his lower body. Its upper leaves wrapped around his head in an affectionate way, almost like it was trying to caress his space helmet.

Strange, provocative, a critic was quoted under the illustration, *unsettling, searching for something*. I'd read a few books by the same author but had never heard of this title before. Above the illustration it read: *on an alien planet, a beautiful and intelligent plant offers more than just companionship...*

I headed towards the register, yanking my wallet out of my pocket. It was love at first sight.

The novel started off with a real humdinger of an opening, a premise fit for the greatest of adventures. A spaceship carrying the universe's most esteemed scientists – it's like a traveling intergalactic symposium but there's also a weird contingency of animal rights activists on board -- collides with a meteor and crash-lands on an unexplored planetoid. The only survivors? A mother and her adult son. They bury the remains of their shipmates and then they set off across a landscape of tropical plants and multicolored stalagmites under a pair of blazing hot suns. They're looking for help, for shelter, for any sign of intelligent life but, unsuccessful and lost, they decide to embark higher into the dangerous ravines.

Halfway up the mountain, they stumble upon their first sign of animal life: *a heavy, harsh but vaguely familiar and fetching odor flying on the wind.*

The son, who has a scientific background in both astronomy and zoology, recognizes the smell.

"Smells like a den of monkeys," he said.

"Are you sure?" his mother asked.

He nodded and headed down the path."One of them is in heat," he added and then took another deep breath through his nose. "Maybe several are."

They climb deeper into the jungle unaware that the monkey-smell is really bait, meant to lure these human primates into the shadows of the canyon. There is the sense that, even if the son did realize the danger, he still wouldn't turn back. The mother becomes concerned. She's never seen this side of him before. He is exhilarated by the smell, by the hunt for its source, and he appears unaware of how excitable he's become. He keeps saying that they're on the verge of discovery. With every step he seems more certain of their future fame and fortune. She listens to his boasts as they hike through the vines and ferns. When they come to the edge of a mossy cliff, he's suddenly whisked away by strong tentacles into the very heart of the mountain.

And here the story takes an interesting and, in the end, a disappointing turn.

Much to my puzzlement, this wasn't the kind of story promised in the cover art or summarized in the blurb. Instead what happens is that the son, for the rest of the novel, is locked away inside the mountain in an embryonic chamber that appears to be alive and intelligent. Like the walls throb to a slow pulse. Female voices sing from the cracks in the stone. Life-affirming waters pool in the corners. It's like he's in the womb of some kind of half-rock half-clam alien. We never see or hear from the mother again, although the son thinks of her a lot. He is certain she would disapprove of his evolving feelings about the walls of his prison, his living rock. It gets a little confusing and complicated toward the end of the seduction but it all leads up to the son participating in a reproductive procedure that, in the novel's final line, begets a litter of cute tiny space scallops.

Closing the book, I felt duped.

I was hoping for a love story between a man and a plant, as advertised, an uninhibited romance between two members of different kingdoms of life, the ultimate taboo. It didn't even matter much to me that the two beings were from two different planets, that the man was an Earthling and the plant an Astrosumerian. What difference would that make? It's the same story here on Spaceship Earth: man and plant worlds apart, two alien species living together but divided by a universe. Man and plant were already engaged in the ultimate long distance relationship.

I'd been trying to figure out a way to cross that distance myself

But so far nothing but strikeouts.

I had yet to figure out a way to convey some message to them, any message. Based on this book cover, I was hoping that Clarissa "Butcher" Cassady had solved the mystery. Her astronaut seemed to have discovered a key into their kingdom that was proving to be elusive to me.

I wanted this book to tell that story: how does one communicate with a tree?

Language would be useless, I supposed. What about grunts, howls, yawps? Would all sounds be useless? Some say music is able to span the gulf between man and plant. Should I hum a tune? Or perhaps gestures would work. Acts of kindness, acts of cruelty, would that compel some sort of response?

Or would it be all about touch?

I was at a loss. I had access to all sorts of tricks, could get my hands on any kind of machinery or magic, yet I could find no way to break a tree's silent spell.

Or what if, this whole time, I was the quiet one? Were the trees trying to communicate with me? How could I receive their messages? Hidden among my many parts and wires, did I have some sort of ancient, dormant radar that could actually pick up a signal from a plant?

How could I turn that on?

I stared at the astronaut on the cover. His hands were clutching the vines that circled his waist. He seemed to be drawing the plant closer to him, a gesture resembling a hug. He had a peculiar smile on his face and his eyes were closed.

I wanted the book to tell that story too.

If I loved a certain plant, how would I know it loved me back? If, for some reason, I found myself alone in the universe, washed ashore and marooned from people, or curtained off from rules and society, would I be bold enough to cast away the taboo and actually embrace a tree?

Would it hug me back?

I felt like the book and that illustration had raised all these questions and promises and, in the end, I was unsatisfied with the answers and the results.

So I stood up, laced up my shoes, folded up my camping chair, got back in the car and back on the road. I would embark on my own adventure. Like that shipwrecked mother and son, I had an unexplored planet too, right at my feet. I also had an undiscovered kingdom living in my midst: the trees, the source of my fascination, the objects of my affection. I could stare at them for hours. I've gone searching for rare and remarkable ones on the mean streets and down the wooded paths. I've kept track of their locations so I could return to them during different parts of the seasons. I've memorized their names and learned how to tell them apart but driving down the highway it occurred to me that not once did I ever get the feeling that they noticed me.

I was shipwrecked too.

My destination was the Schuylkill Center, 340 acres of parkland on the outskirts of the Roxborough neighborhood, about as far west as you can stand and still be in Philadelphia. My friend Gina had an uncertified organic farm there, about an acre and a

A common sight while walking the Pine Grove Loop, retired farm-land in transition to woodland; first colonizers like crabgrass, black walnut, and sassafras are called pioneer species.

half off Hagy's Mill Road. West of the farm, there was a visitor center, a giant greenhouse, and a pre-school that also served as headquarters for a summer camp. Somewhere to the south, there was a small wildlife clinic. From Gina's gate, the main trail followed the edges of meadows, ponds, and streams small enough to be called *runs*. The rest was forest, most of it twentieth-century pastureland gone wild.

Over the years it's become my favorite place for a hike: a combination of a young wood full of crabapple, dogwood, redbud, and sassafras and a much older forest that lies in the middle of the Center. The hike through the younger population of trees towards that inner forest was like walking backwards through the history of the land.

At first everything feels young and short and full of light, the sunshine breaking through the low ceiling of all those small understory trees. There's lots of space in between the trunks so plenty of room for native forbs, thistles and graminoids like

The Ravine Loop cuts a path through a more mature, more stable forest characterized by larger, taller trees that establish canopies, or stories, for the wildlife.

the yarrow, the stinging nettle, and the mayapple, which if I remember right the turtles should be feasting on by this time of year. Deeper down the trail, over there in mountain laurel country, the creeks crack the hillside into a steep ravine. That's where the older forest begins to show its face. Grass gives way to moss, sunshine turns to mist as you enter the antique land. Clear streams roll and tumble in between the rocky hills. Along the trail there are signs of contemporary industrial infrastructure, mostly pipes, lying there among the rocks and trees like futuristic fossils. The bridges over the creeks always have spots in need of fixing, different spots each time, the constant work of the Great Repairer, spirit keeper of this trail. As you walk among the bigger trees the roof of the forest will keep rising and the trail keeps plunging deeper into a dark, steamy, sylvan land of sycamore, maple, oak, tulip poplar and -- my prey for the afternoon -- the beech tree.

The great tree writer Donald Culross Peattie once wrote: *A beech is, in almost any landscape where it appears, the finest tree to be seen.*

But with all due respect to Donald Culross Peattie I'd had enough with the seeing. The time had come for conversation and I was finally ready to make the first move.

On Hagy's Mill Road, about a half-mile before the Center's main entrance, there was a sandlot that Gina used for parking. Normally a little muddy, today it was dry and slippery and I skidded to a stop in a cloud of brown dust.

I jumped out the car and rummaged through the trunk, looking for any tools or equipment that might be helpful for the mission. I dropped the items into a pile at my feet: a tape measure, a mason jar, a pair of binoculars, and my favorite flashlight. I'd left my backpack at home but I found a reusable bag under the passenger seat, something I must've purchased at one of the supermarkets. Each side of the bag had these really lame photo collages of downtown Philadelphia, the skyscrapers, the Rocky statue, the Liberty Bell, the stadiums, and the statue of William Penn on top of City Hall.

This was the absolute worst kind of camouflage for the woods, I thought, but I had no other choice.

Right before closing the trunk, after careful consideration, I grabbed the jumper cables and dropped them into the shopping bag with the other supplies.

I was hoping Gina would be at the farm so I could stop in for a brief hello, as one is wont to do when it comes to farmers, but her van wasn't in the sandlot. This wasn't completely out of the ordinary. She did have a weakness for the burritos across the highway in the Andorra Shopping Center. Or the van could be parked inside the farm. Gina used it sometimes like a giant wheelbarrow.

I walked on the path towards her gate and peered through the links of her deer fencing. I could hear the chickens on the other side of the rows but only the top of the coop was visible. I dug out the binoculars and scanned the distance for any sign of Gina and her van. There really wasn't that much to see from this side of the gate, although I was enjoying how different the farm looked in close-up through the binoculars. The way the air above her garden was cloudy with bugs, the row of poblano peppers swinging like lanterns, eggplants as black blobs, every peach a Jupiter.

I could tell Gina wasn't there by the crows. They were walking down her field, pecking at the summer squash, something Gina would never tolerate.

Her absence was unfortunate but I knew it would only serve as an advantage for the hunt. I had managed to make it this far into the day without speaking to anybody at all. I hadn't really seen or heard from anybody either, unless you counted the Car People I passed along the highway. At this point any human contact had to be considered a risk, a taint. No matter how friendly or brief the visit, the human world always found a way to cling to my clothes, play itself on repeat inside my head, and scare away the trees.

I was only at the edge of their woods but I already felt surrounded, and inhabited, by a profound, primitive silence, something that would prove to be more useful than any tool I carried in my shopping bag.

Thoreau once wrote: *I frequently tramped eight or ten miles through the deepest snow to keep an appointment with a beech-tree.*

My journey would be a lot less miles but I was still impatient. I didn't want to lose the momentum or lose the nerve. I stepped away from Gina's gate and headed down the trail with an extra step in my stride. Perhaps today was the day. Perhaps I was the guy, first man to talk tree.

And there was no doubt in my mind which tree it should be.

From her gate, the trail made a dramatic glide into the younger wood and I blended right into its dappled shade. Birdsong announced my entrance. The eavesdropper had arrived. I walked right by the white pine grove, normally a pitstop on my hikes here, and tramped as fast as I could through the first series of meadows.

Usually when I'm searching and hunting down a specific Philly tree, I'm inside the actual city surrounded by my people. My turf, I guess you could say. Trying to track down a tree in the woods was a entirely different story and required a different set of operational and observational skills. I was in their kingdom now. Despite my knowledge of their names and characteristics, I walked through their midst as an outsider, bouncing down their grid with my noisy human being, my big brain, and these strange legs. Did they ever get used to such monstrosity? They reached into the trail to scratch at my skin, such soft human bark.

It gave me an odd feeling, like I didn't belong here today, like maybe I forgot this was a day-off for the trees too and I was being rude, entitled, bossy.

The shopping bag wasn't helping either. The contents clanged together with every bad step. I tried holding it against my chest and wrapping my arms around it. That made it a little quieter but when I looked down at all those stupid Philly photos I felt like an even bigger bumpkin.

I was walking through the woods like a billboard for Philadelphia.

The next part of the trail was just up ahead and it began with a slow descent through dogwood and elder to the Wind Dance Pond, a big barrel of green water surrounded by sycamores and cattails. I jumped down the last few steps of the hill and walked along the water's edge, frogs a-leaping with every stomp of my foot. On the other side of the pond, I used a big block of exposed quartz as a step into the woods and picked up the the trail again. From here the trail followed Smith Creek upstream into the oldest part of the forest.

I would be in the heart of it soon, a city of a million trees, but there was really only one tree I had in mind.

All things considered, the beech has got to be one of the most familiar trees in the entire country, if not the world. Even if the average citizen didn't know its proper name they would still recognize its appearance. For many purposes, it is the epitome of the deciduous hardwood tree. That's why it's found frequently throughout childhood inside primers and picture books, or part of the set for a childrens' play. It's the kind of tree you grow up with. It's found later in life silhouetted into logos and letterheads. It is, I believe, the tree in the Planet Petco logo and I hope one day to prove that true. It's also found ubiquitously in our literature. Famous scenes from our imagination have taken place among the beeches. Jason retrieved the Golden Fleece from the branches of a beech tree, one guarded by a sleepless blue-eyed serpent. Later on in the 5th Century, the beeches are listed among the first wave of attackers in the Druid poem, *Cad Goddeu, The Battle of the Trees*. Much later, the Merry Men would rally around them in Sherwood Forest, their rebel tree-houses concealed among their boughs. In other beech forests, always be on the lookout for hobbits hiding in their roots, breathlessly waiting for the Black Riders to pass.

I couldn't help but hope that perhaps one day this adventure of mine will also be included in its legendarium, wherever tales of beech-trees are still sung.

But as I followed the switchbacks down the hillside, little moments of doubt surfaced to the top of my thoughts. Was this even possible? That was the big question. To talk to a tree?

Based on everything I'd been reading lately, I was convinced it was still within the realm of possibilities. After all, we already know they're talking to each other. They're using the underground mycelium threads from the fungus kingdom to connect their root tips. Once connected, the larger, older, mother trees transfer water and nutrients, especially carbon, to the younger, smaller trees in their web. Any given mother tree will favor their own descendants over any other tree that latches on to their mycelium but it's definitely a system that encourages cooperation over competition. In exchange for using their threads as a means of transport, the mycelium absorb a good chunk of the trees' stock of sugar, which is a byproduct of photosynthesis. It's called the *mycorrhizal network*, or the *wood-wide web*.

Those same connections are used to exchange more than just nutrients and sugar. The trees also use them as a way to communicate with each other, especially to transfer useful knowledge, like when a mother tree helps the younger trees identify a particular insect that's on the attack. The mother tree will send its group the necessary chemicals to change the flavor of their bark and leaves, making themselves unappetizing to the current bug. Other studies have shown that trees will also use phermones as an alarm system, expelling specific compositions of gas to its neighbors to warn them of the danger. One forester in Germany talks about how some trees will fling a cloud of phermones into the forest that, once sniffed, would attract the current pest's natural enemies, who are hopefully passing through the area downwind.

All these forms of communication, I thought, happening all around me, underneath me, flying over my head, and I can't hear or smell a thing. First step to real contact could be a matter of just finding a way to interrupt the conversation.

Or to block it all together. That would get their attention.

I reached into the shopping bag to touch the jumper cables, ran my finger down the clamp's cold, sharp teeth. Every attempt to intercept their messages had failed in the past but today I was prepared to take a more forceful approach, a louder strategy.

Further into the woods, the path veered away from the creek and began a steep rise towards a cleft in the ravine. As I began the ascent, I noticed my first beeches of the day. They were thin and straight and grouped together in tight formations. As I climbed higher they grew further apart from each other, getting stouter and taller the closer I got to the top, until right at the crest of the hill there stood the thickest, tallest, weirdest one of the whole grove. Its position on top of the hill seemed to cast the entire woods in its shade, mother of the mountain.

Compared to all the other trees of the woods, the beech is the easiest to identify. There's never any need to look for its fruit, memorize its leaf, or study its twig. Identification begins with either a nod towards its famous roots, the way they rip across the forest floor sprouting other trees along the way, or with a long gaze into its distinct, beautiful, mesmerizing bark, the way it wraps around the tree like a tight sheet. The bark is often described as *smooth* but I know it as a gritty, wrinkled skin, more canvas than silk. The novice observer calls the color *gray* but a closer look will reveal a silver-streaked landscape: shades of oyster and lead, the polished chrome, speckled green from the moss. At night it lights up the path in shades of blue pearl. It's unlike any other tree and maybe that's why it stands the most apart. Even when surrounded by the other giants of the forest, the beech will always seem to live a separate solitary sort of life, aloof to any drama or competition. It follows a slower calendar and seems to cast a more private, though friendly, curtain of shade, more monk than king.

The beech, Donald Culross Peattie once wrote, *is all that we want a tree to be.*

Well, we shall see about that, Mr. Culross Peattie.

And just then Gina must've returned to the farm, seen my car parked in the sandlot, and sent me a text message. I pulled my phone from my pocket but I instantly regretted the move. I could

From Penn State Extension: "It is a climax species and may be a predominant species in a forest...In the wild, American beech often forms dense colonies by suckering up from its shallow roots."

feel all the beeches receding from the sound of the message's buzz, could sense them flinching at the glow of my phone's artificial light. Whatever eyes they'd been using to watch me hike through their kingdom, the trees now scuttled them up their trunks to a higher, safer distance and gazed at me with suspicion through the screen of their twigs and leaves.

Where you at, Gina had sent.

But at the present moment that wasn't such an easy question for me to answer.

TO BE CONTINUED*...stay tuned for the thrilling conclusion to the beech chapter. Will our intrepid narrator finally make first contact? Or has Gina ruined the mood yet again? Open the pod bay doors and set the phasers to stun. This is a diplomatic mission into the very heart of the tree kingdom. Spoiler alert: he's been on the planet of the apes the entire time.*

It's not true but, in some field guides, you'll see the claim that the words "beech" and "book" share the same Germanic root word; some of mankind's earliest writing tablets were made of beech bark, a tradition that unfortunately continues today.

Two more notable Philadelphia beeches: (above) at Frankford Ave. and Ashburner St. near the historic King's Highway Bridge; (below) The Great Beech in the Andorra Farm section of the Wissahickon, a state champion, over 110 ft tall, over 150 years old.

Based on my own observations and travels, the two most frequently cited words carved into Philadelphia beeches: (1) my brother Joey's name, and (2) Led Zeppelin, also seen as Led Zep, or Zofo.

Black locust

According to the fossil record, the black locusts were almost completely wiped out during the last Ice Age. The few surviving populations found safe harbor from the glaciers atop the plateaus of the Ozark Mountains in present-day Arkansas and Missouri and that's where they stayed for thousands of years. When the ice finally retreated, the black locusts went back on the march, down the walls of the plateaus and back into the forests, just in time for the Age of Mega-Mammals. Look for small woody spikes at the base of its twigs and leaves. Those spikes are relics from that ancient era. Now obsolete, they were once a weapon against woolly mammoths, short-faced bears, cave lions and their ilk. They still appear in pairs on the tree, sharp as ever.

The next surges in the black locust population involved the participation of human hands, not so mega a mammal back then. First up were the Indians who transplanted the black locust from the forests into the areas surrounding their village commons, in the meadows and coastal plains of Appalachia. They propagated the black locust to have a constant supply of good wood for their homes, buildings, wagons, fencing, and bows for bows and arrows. Records show that this wood was used by the Virginia

Company to build Jamestown, the first English settlement. Future colonists took the tree to the next level and moved them right into the other Jimmytowns popping up on the piedmont. History books note that it was first used as a street tree in 1730s Virginia. I can't find any record that pinpoints exactly when first it was used on the streets of Philadelphia but – and I honestly have no idea how true this next part is – it must've already been a familiar tree when William Penn and Thomas Holme planned out the original city grid, which always included a Locust Street.

It's known as an aggressive grower, especially when stressed, a survival skill I like to imagine it developed when battling extinction atop the plateaus. In the forestry textbooks it's labeled as a member of the *pioneer species*, one that prefers the edges of disturbed woods or the sunny spaces of old fields, retired farms, and abandoned construction zones. In certain parts of the megalopolis it pops up uninvited along the highways and inside the parks. Now it sometimes comes with a warning: *potentially invasive*, which is not too bad considering how close we came to losing the tree altogether.

It's hard for me to picture the black locust so vulnerable and so close to the brink of extinction. I know it as a very brawny, very sturdy tree. In my travels I've noticed that most of them grow into three kinds of shapes: (1) a single straight muscular trunk, or (2) a trunk that splits into several arms at the base of its trunk or (2b) that splits halfway up the trunk in the arms of a Y, or (3) a pagoda style with lots of crooked and drooping branches. I love its bark, one of the Top Five Barks of All-Time, super-ropy, the corduroy of trees, the strands of its weave so thick that I can actually clench the cords in my hands. I can literally grab the tree. The color is usually gray, sometimes silver, but as it ages the bark peels and unravels around the edges revealing a reddish-brown fray.

Beneath that bark is the most durable and hardest wood in all of Turtle Island, notorious for dulling saws and axes. It's perfect for firewood, doesn't need to be cured or kiln-dried, with BTUs high enough that once alight it burns with a blue flame. One time at the Clark Park farmers' market, I pointed out a black locust to Mr. Bimmerstock when he was on his break. He was leaning on the construction fence across the street from his fruit stand eating his sandwich. The black locust was growing on the other side of the construction fence leaning over Mr. Bimmerstock. He said he'd heard of the tree but knew it only as a post tree, it being the first choice for fence posts out in the country. He's right. It's also the first choice for railroad ties. During the 1800s, the shipwrights began using black locust pegs for nails when building the American Navy, replacing iron bolts. You might think that all this strength comes from age but the black locust is just a fast grower with a short, virile life, rare to reach a hundred years old.

They are discovered along the borders of the Philly woods reliably, most often found creeping along the first half-mile of any trail. I rarely find black locust deep within the forest. It's a rare street tree but there are some very cool ones downtown; one of my favorites is at the Benjamin Rush House, 3rd and Walnut. I've also found some real spooky ones, tall and twisted, in the Germantown and Chestnut Hill cemeteries.

Impressive black locust at the historic Benjamin Rush House at 3rd & Walnut Streets around the corner from America's first bank.

The leaflets are a dull green, small and oval with smooth edges. They remind me of sequins but not as shiny. They are very patient, almost the last to leaf out for the summer. At night they fold up as if going to sleep. No one knows exactly why. By late November, the leaves ripen to a plain yellow but if there's a frost before Thanksgiving they will fall off still green. Its fruit is a short brown pea pod that tends to persist and hang on the branches all winter long. Inside the pods are four to eight black peas, how it earned the name *black locust.*

The fans of the black locust have probably figured out by now that I'm saving the best feature for last: those beautiful, plentiful, and festive flowers. They grow in tassels, drooping between the sequined leaves, growing in tassels. Think wisteria, think wind chimes. Individual flowers are soft and spongy, very expressive like an orchid, and a real pleasing milky white. Most remarkably, they open up all at once, like a chain reaction, not just every flower on a single tree but every black locust in the city all at the same time. It's a joyous habit for a living creature to share with the world, one instantaneous citywide crop of flowers. It reminds us how common it is, how it's been lurking in the shadows the whole time. That's when I remember how much the tree means to me, seeing the tassels christening the cliffs of 76, or blazing inside the woody shoulders of Roosevelt Boulevard, or dangling into the sunshine over the hairpin turns of Lincoln Drive, popping out of the understory everywhere I go under the Strawberry Moon.

I didn't even know they were edible until I saw Chef Bobby sprinkle some on top of a salad at his South Philly BYO. They're tasty, with a touch of honey, a hint of orange and one good crunch before it melts away on the tongue.

One year later I saw Chef Bobby at the Clark Park farmers' market and I told him that the black locusts were in bloom again, was wondering if he'd put them on his menu like before. He was up for it and asked me to take him to a tree. I walked him across the street to the one behind the construction fence but its flowers were too high to harvest.

I offered to take him to a street tree further into the neighborhood, one I passed the other day that I'd never noticed before. I recalled its plentiful display of flowers and thought it'd be a good one to forage from. He led me to his car which was parked around the corner from the market. I was happy to play hooky from work for a while but I wasn't entirely confident I could remember the exact address of the tree and, in fact, my first guess was wrong, and my second guess too.

"I'm short on time," Chef Bobby said. "I thought you knew where it was."

"It's not my fault," I told him. "The trees move around too much."

Eventually I did find the tree I was hunting for but we had to park down the street from it. He dug into his trunk, found a paring knife, and we walked the two blocks distance back to the black locust. As he walked around it, he clipped off tassels of flowers and handed the harvest to me. I cradled them in my arms until he was done. As we headed back to his car, people stared at us. We noticed but it just made us laugh. He opened his back door, found some newspaper on the floor, smoothed it out and laid it down on the back seat. I stood there, trying not to let any tassels fall through my arms. I was careful not to handle the flowers too roughly or to press them too tightly against my chest. He reached into the harvest. He pinched a tassel from its cut end and shrugged off the other tassels that clung to it. He laid each one gently and gingerly onto the newspaper. The way the flowers went from my arms into the back seat of his vehicle, I felt like we were passing between us some long-lost treasure found at last.

BLOODROOT

Unforgettable but easy to miss, the bloodroot have a cult status among the other creatures of the woods and, for many of us here in the city, they're the catch of the season. They live right below the surface, at most five inches underfoot. That's really not a meaningful distance from our own world but the bloodroot are strange enough to make it feel like a million miles. In many aspects, they're the plant version of the mole rat, the spirit vegetable to the earthworm. The bloodroot exist at that same silent, furtive, nether level.

It's got to be one of the most basic lifeforms ever: a buried stem only a few inches long. The stem burrows through the subsoil by growing nodes. I'm tempted to describe how it burrows using the word *horizontally* but there are no horizons on the bloodroot's planet. Best to quote the botany books: *growing perpendicular to gravity*. According to legend, some Indian tribes used the stem to induce abortions. Other Indian tribes used it to dye their clothes and weapons. When dug up, most people will say it looks like ginger except for their bright red and orange colors. Slice them open and they'll start dripping sap the color of beet juice. That's why we call them *bloodroot*.

The anatomy for this creature stays pretty simple. It's the stem, it's them nodes, and then usually one leaf and one flower per node. All of the action happens at the nodes. By action, I mean the growing of two very thin stalks erupting through the skin of the node like an eye growing off a potato. The stalks tunnel through the soil up towards the walking world. One stalk holds the bud that contains the flower. The other stalk is the petiole that will become the leaf. They breach the surface of the earth at the same moment. Eventually the leaf will completely unfurl but for the first few moments it stays in a protective gesture curled around its sister-stalk. She's getting ready to flower. We only know where the bloodroot are by those flowers.

Petals are big, bold and showy, the hottest white, and usually eight in number. The center of the flower is a bright golden button. They are found very low to ground, at most two inches above the woodland floor. They are never alone. They live in groups called *colonies*. Sometimes these colonies are next to other colonies but usually they're separated by some larger structure, like a big boulder or a great beech, or they're on the opposite banks of a creek, or they're just further down the trail glowing in the distance. Once locked in, your eyes keep noticing new colonies. According to the field guides, the bloodroot love a good hill, something to do with well-drained soil, but I've found some colonies here in the city what've settled in a flatland or nested in the mud.

Their native range is enormous: the entire eastern coast from Florida to Nova Scotia, the complete Mississippi River valley and the entire midwest, and all the way north to the Hudson Bay. Interesting to see on the map, their full range ends as a dead stop in the middle of the continent. Nothing at all west of the Great Plains. I guess they haven't found a way to tunnel through the Rockies yet.

I follow certain blogs and I like certain Facebook pages just to hear word of the bloodroot. When the flowers come scrolling up the newsfeed, it's game on, a sudden sick day, and a dash out the door. Their whole season is a blink: one, two days tops, very early in the season, and yet their magic can last the entire year, its own perennial. For that brief time, they kindly turn the still-wintered woods into a storybook. This is our native poppy and the most wild of our wildflowers.

I live near a great gathering of their colonies and that makes me feel very lucky. It's only four miles away, inside Morris Park of the Overbrook neighborhood. This is not your typical city park. For starters, it's bigger than most, 190 acres, which makes it number nine on the list of Philadelphia's largest parks. It's located along the western boundary of the city map between Lansdowne Avenue and City Avenue. If you cross City Ave, you're outside the city all together. This is border country. Looking at the shape of the entire park on the computer map, it looks like a green Y, but more like a lowercase y. There's a giant playground at the bottom of that y, called Papa Playground. That's the only real structure. The rest of the park is a walk through a dense forest. Inside that forest there are two branches of the Indian Creek, each branch a stem of that y. The creeks converge inside Morris Park around 68th Street. It's my favorite part of the entire Overbrook neighborhood, a meeting of the waters unlike any other in the city, just happening all the time day and night right behind the row of homes on 68th Street. To arrive at that meeting place, you must first find passage between those homes and then find the right paths through the crowded, slanted corridors of familiar trees, like oaks, maples, tulip poplars, sycamores, beeches, and just enough ashes and hemlocks to turn this giant backyard into one big patch of true blue Pennsylvania woods.

I visit once a year to catch the bloodroot. Catch them if I can. Some years I'm too late. Some years, by the time I even get the news and get to the park, the flowers are already gone and the green seedpod is already hanging from the stalks. Show over. Another unremarkable year has begun.

But arriving on time is more challenging than it sounds. Exact dates for the bloom are impossible to predict and please don't believe anybody who says they know for sure. You can't rely on the blogs and the Facebook feeds either. Photos are usually one day old and that's one day closer to goodbye, better luck next year. What is the trigger that begins the flowering? Is it temperature, tilt of earth, length of day? No one knows. One thing is for sure: it has to happen before Morris Park leafs out. The bloodroot need to do all their blooming and fruiting before the big trees can block their sun. That's the deadline. Then the only wise answer is a range: third week of March to the second weekend in April, to be on the safe side. But that's not even foolproof. There was one time when they didn't bloom until April 18th. Everybody thought they'd missed them for the year and then they just show up, out of the blue. The year before that, they were open and closed by April 4th and that was the year we were coming out of a record-breaking winter. Morris Park was still fleeced with snow.

The first time I went hunting for bloodroot I found them on March 29th, which was definitely on the earlier side of their typical season, although I do remember how impatient I was for them to arrive. I'd been hunting them every day since the 21st. This was during a period of my life notable for long swaths of terrific leisure, entire afternoons as empty as the Void. I'd been laid off since January and was finally getting the hang of it. First day of the hunt was frigid and icy. Knowing that I was early in the season, I spent the bitter hours getting the lay of the land. A stranger to Morris Park, I was impressed by how quickly the woods deepened. I was barely inside the park and it already felt like the heart of a forest. The creeks were running a bright white from the melting snow. Only when hiking closer to City Ave did one hear the presence of a more advanced society, in this case the Car People stuck in traffic. By the end of day two, temperatures reached a level high enough to begin the Great Thaw and on day three I found heads of skunk cabbage rising from the mud of the West Branch Indian Creek.

Day four was the dead deer. I didn't even see it at first. I was walking along the main trail about to climb the hill towards City Ave and it was lying on top of the big rock in the middle of the creek. It blended right into the gray and dun world of the Marchland. It was splayed over the entire rock, a pose that told the tale of its final minutes: a crash on the highway, maybe the shattering of a headlight, the sound of hooves on black ice. The deer leaps over the safety rails over the cobblestone culvert. It falls through the air and belly flops on the boulder in the middle of the Indian. Deer ribs cracking. The hind legs dip into the creek, the current runs through the deer hair, the broken head gazes downstream. I walked to the edge of the creek and jumped from stone to stone to get closer to the kill, fresh blood on the bloodroot trail. The other side of the creek was carpeted with the flowers of yellow celandine, another first sign of spring. On my way out of Morris Park on day six, I found a dead snake.

"What the hell is going on in that park?" Goldberg asked.

"Dead snake," I said again. "It was just lying there in the center of the trail. True story."

"How did it die?"

"No idea," I said, "and why was it just lying there in the trail like that? It's the strangest thing, right there in the middle of the trail stretched out from head to toe."

I didn't get into it with Goldberg at that moment but, actually, the strangest part was that I'd just walked that trail only an hour ago and there was no dead snake. I spent most of that hour sitting on a log watching the creek flow past me and I found the dead snake on the way back down the same trail.

"It's an omen," Goldberg said.

"I feel the same way."

"Are you going back there tomorrow?" he asked.

"I think tomorrow's the day. Come with me."

Goldberg laughed. "You're too early and it's still too cold. I'm not wasting the day off."

"Tomorrow's the day," I said.

But it was actually the day after tomorrow when the bloodroot finally flowered. I swear I knew something was different the moment I stepped into Morris Park. They were so much smaller than I expected. I wanted to take off my shoes for fear I'd do some damage to them, clodhopper that I am. Every flower was like a little periscope connected to the stem buried below the surface.

"Happy arrival day," I said, quoting Sun Ra.

I knelt down on the ground, my knees sinking into the mud. I wasn't expecting how beautiful they would be, alive and in person. I was bowed to their beauty. In their presence I never before felt so rough, so ugly. Compared to the bloodroot, I was a beast and a brute with a reckless appetite for time. What would I do differently if I had only one day in the sun? Why do I think there will always be more time? I said to myself: be like the bloodroot for by tomorrow this flower will be gone and by this day next week the green seedpod will be hanging from the stalk. When ripe, those seedpods are harvested by armies of carpenter ants. They only eat the pulp inside those pods, not the seeds. The seeds end up discarded in an anthill's equivalent to a trash chamber room, from whence the next generation of bloodroot come to life. That's why they grow in colonies.

Leaving Morris Park later that day, my mind was already racing towards tomorrow, to all the tomorrows that now stood between this day and the next day the bloodroot blooms. I call it a *day*, as if I am with them for an entire day, but when it comes to the bloodroot I should really count that time by the hours. How many hours per year do I spend with the bloodroot? Maybe two hours, at most three hours per arrival day. How many other days are there in between those hours? Three hundred? Three fifty? If I'm not careful, if I don't stay alert, then it could be years in between those hours. How many times would it take for all those hours to add up to a full day? How many years will there be in that day? Why do those years flow by so fast?

*Pyrus calleryana slowly falling over at 18th and Wallace Streets,
Fairmount neighborhood, one fine spring day.*

CALLERY PEAR

Walking out the front door of my urban cabin, no matter which way I turn, it won't be too long before I bump into one of those controversial callery pears. If I turn west, then I meet my first one right on the corner, standing next to the Springfield Avenue traffic light. It's big enough and tall enough for me to assume it's at the end of its lifespan. That makes it around twenty years old. The neighborhood's changed a lot in those twenty years, the tree as well. What was once a good, tight, handsome, egg-shaped crown is now one huge shaggy mess. The tree has cracked open and it can't be put together again. High above, the branches are buckling under their own weight, swaying at dangerous angles, and it's only a matter of time before it all comes crashing down on some poor car or some poor soul. It's the typical fate of the older callery pears. Knowing my luck, I'll be stuck at the red light when it happens.

Still heading west, there's another pear right after that one. It's just as tall and just as old but it's been shorn away from the wires, looks like a tree missing its other half.

If I turn east from my front door, then the nearest pear is across 46th Street in front of the garage doors of Wayne's Garage.

This pear is only a stump with a few struggling twigs hanging off what's left of its trunk. The rest of the tree was blowed down during a snowstorm many years ago. It still has some life in its engine though. Every late March or early April, this stump twinkles with white flowers like all the other pears in this city.

I'm pretty sure most people in Philadelphia are like me, surrounded by callery pears. Depending on the neighborhood you could be boxed in even more. For example, I once read a tree survey that counted all the trees in the 3.5-square-mile grid between Snyder and Oregon Avenues east of Broad. The callery pear came in fourth: cherry, maple, sycamore, callery pear.

My little hideout in West Philly isn't as crowded as that section of South Philly but there are still plenty of those calleryana lurking around. When I stop to think about it, they've been lurking around me my whole life, going all the way back to my childhood home. There used to be four of them inside the cul-de-sac where I grew up, a pear for every house.

I can still remember the day they arrived. I was watching from the window, a good, tight, handsome, egg-shaped tree myself. They came rolling into the court in the back of a pickup truck, their roots bundled up in burlap bags, the new kids on the block. They were but saplings, young and frail, but each one was already beaming with a bright perfect crown. They looked like green lollipops. One by one, they were dropped into place in the grassy strip between sidewalk and curb, potato sack and all. They looked even smaller once in the ground. For most of that year they were tied up to training posts. I remember my father explaining how important it was to keep the knots on the training posts tight and secure, how the ropes tugging on each side of the tree helped it grow straight. The pear in front of my house grew up to become first base.

No when I flip through the old family albums, I notice that pear in the background of the photos. It's standing next to me as

I'm waving goodbye about to get on the bus for my first day of kindergarten. It's there when I was coasting down the driveway on my first solo bike ride. It's part of the Fourth of July picnics on the front yard. It's posing next to me and Goldberg and our senior prom dates and, only months later, leaning over my first car parked in its shade and packed to the gills the morning I left for college. Flipping through the photos, I can watch all the pears in that cul-de-sac growing up in unison, year after year reaching the same heights and replicating the same exact shape as the others, good clones that they were.

There is a part of me now that is repulsed by that clone-ness, for that kind of unnatural engineering, and by their uniformity and ubiquity, but those weren't the kinds of qualities that I really noticed as a kid. And I wouldn't have felt any repulsion even if I did notice those traits in the pears. At that time in my life I was also trying to be the same clone as everyone else.

And there's no way I could've known this but the same exact scenes were playing out in neighborhoods just like mine all over the country. In fact, it'd been happening for decades, since the 1950s when the first clones were delivered to a brand new suburb outside Washington, D.C., although some people claim they'd didn't technically debut to the public until 1963, the year the callery pear made the cover of the American Nurseryman magazine. By the time they arrived on my block, the clones had a population over ten thousand strong with a range that put them in just about every town and city from coast to coast.

It was a nationwide fad and, like other fads from that era, like Silly Putty and LSD, its roots are found inside that most unlikely of sources: the U.S. Government.

It was toward the end of the Second Industrial Revolution, during those first few years of the Machine Age, early 20th-Century according to the almanac, with yet another terrible tragedy befalling the American farmer. In this case, it was the pear farmers of the Pacific Northwest. A deadly blight was ripping through their orchards, rows and rows of dying pear trees as far as the eye could see.

To the rescue, the US Department of Agriculture summoned the most popular, most intrepid tree-hunters of the day and set them loose around the world. Their mission: find a pear that could withstand the blight on its own. Go wherever pears grow on this planet and find some tenacious little bugger with a natural immunity against the deadly mildew and send us back as many shoots, roots, and seeds as you can muster. With your help, the botanists here at home could take those pear genes and -- theoretically -- breed a whole new and improved race of fruit-bearing trees.

Bring back the world's strongest pear and save the orchards.

It was Frank Meyer, of Meyer lemon fame, already a renowned tree-hunter but with a reputation as a man of restless disposition, who hit the jackpot south of the Yangtze River in the unexplored mountains of Shanghai province.

Pyrus calleryana is simply a marvel, Frank Meyer wrote in one of his letters back to the Department. *One finds it growing in all sorts of conditions.*

He went deep into the Chinese backcountry. For years, his only contact with the modern world was the series of letters he exchanged with his USDA counterpart back in Washington. Toward the end, his correspondences often included signs of depression and half-hearted resignations.

I often think, he wrote, *the life I am leading here is perhaps not the thing I ought to continue much longer.*

And yet he continued to hunt down and ship back as many of those tiny pears as he could find. The USDA went to work on them immediately. Within a few years, they had thousands of seedlings growing inside the Plant Introduction Station of Glenn

(left) *Photograph of Frank N. Meyer (1875-1918) Department of Agriculture explorer; The World Today Magazine, Nov 1909*

(right) *From Dept. of Agriculture collection, "Shrub Habit with Frank Meyer (18 Feb. 1911)."*

Frank Meyer's note: "On some places in the desert where the water was near the surface, we passed through veritable jungles of Tamarisk bushes. Sometimes they were up to 20 ft. tall and had stems 1/2 ft. in diameter."

Dale, Maryland, one of their new experimental nurseries, this one located in the suburbs of Washington, D.C.

For some reason I always imagine the experimental nursery as a top-secret operation, the kind that's hidden from the books. It's built like a military base with a set of barracks around the perimeter and one large cafeteria for everyone. Security is lax all over the operation but that seems to be okay. There aren't many people trying to get into the Glenn Dale Plant Introduction Station. Nobody is trying to escape either, although that doesn't explain why I always picture in the background of this imaginarium the silhouettes of guard towers.

In the center of the station, the pear trees grow in long, straight rows. They are under observation at all times. Everything about them is measured and tested. In my mind's eye, the nursery is always stirring with teams of farmers and botanists. Some are wearing white lab coats buttoned up over khaki uniforms. Some show up to work wearing pleated suits or skirts, others in overalls or dungarees. They buzz around the secret orchard studying the trees with a childlike sense of wonder.

And I'm not sure why but whenever I stop and think about those farmers and scientists my mind's eye paints the scenery with a sentimental, sappy brush. The longer I linger inside this nostalgium, the more childlike the scientists act and the more contagious the sense of wonder. Their youthful nature transforms them into the same age I was when those pears arrived in my cul-de-sac, and then they are transformed again into the same kids that grew up with me in that old neighborhood.

We must've been drafted into government service but we're having the time of our lives, reunited for one more adventure. During the day we scurry up and down the pear rows taking notes on our clipboards. When it's raining we're stuck inside the classroom typing up our results. Some of us get too attached to certain trees, always a heartbreaking scene when it's harvested for the latest experiment. At night we sneak out of the barracks and rendezvous in the heart of the orchard and play in the dark. When the trees bloom for those two weeks in early spring, the entire experiment slows to a crawl. We wander under the trees and never think of growing up and leaving the nursery but always out there on the horizon: the generals in their jeeps watching the experimental trees and us lab animals through their giant binoculars.

"Pretty flowers," one of them says, "but can they grow a real pear?"

The answer was no. The calleries were able to resist the blight but they couldn't graft well enough to grow any pear worth producing for the public market. Eventually, the Pacific Northwest crop was saved by other advances in the field of horticulture and plant husbandry but the overall mission and the long experiment wasn't all in vain. Sometime in the middle of the 1950s, the USDA finally figured out exactly what Frank Meyer had discovered out there in the wilds.

This is the story's final bitter twist, the ironic epilogue to Frank Meyer's biography.

Because here was one of the most fearless tree-hunters ever, renowned for his ability to walk through hundreds of miles of uncharted territory, with over 200 discoveries attributed to his expeditions, including the seedless persimmon and the first oil-bearing soybean, but in the end the joke's on him. Coyote always gets the last laugh. Because it turns out Frank Meyer spent all those years exploring the wilds only to end up hunting down the perfect street tree.

Over the years his discovery has had a lot of ups and downs, more than most trees. By the time I was learning about it in my freshman year dendrology course, its reputation among professors and tree-hunters was at rock bottom and yet its reputation among city planners and the general public was still peaking. This would be in the late 1990s, at the beginning of the First Cyber Revolution, the dawn of the Age of Disconnected Networks. At college, the most popular majors seemed to be Computer Science and Communications. I was an English major taking Natural Resource Management courses on the side. I was the only English major among future botanists, park rangers, landscape architects, and environmental scientists.

"Because I like trees," was my answer in front of the entire class when my professor asked what an English major was doing in his Dendrology 101 course.

After the other students got done laughing, he looked me straight in the eyes and said, "I like trees too."

A few weeks later he included the callery pear in his lecture about popular street trees. He portrayed the tree in a negative light, as was the custom at the time. You could almost say we were taught to despise it.

I was thrilled to join the bandwagon. At that time in my life I already had a long list of popular things I loved to hate.

(above and right) *Photos taken on the same day two miles apart.*

The callery pear was the perfect addition. It represented my entire litany of sins and vices: commercialization, conformity, monotony, government overreach, cultural and botanical misappropriation. It was a tree as product, bred to please the public at the risk of its own health, one that was cloned for the rat race and cultivated to the point of mass production.

I was still a young man, resolved to avoid that fate myself.

Since those university days, I bet I've heard every argument for and against its propagation and circulation. I know I've heard all the names: a horticultural dead end, an ornamental cookie cutter, a frankentree. And yet for this present moment count me down as one of its defenders. I'm a fan, for now. It's a surprise even to myself but lately my gut instinct tells me to stick up for the guy, although I'm not sure if that's because I've actually gotten to like the tree or because I still enjoy going against the grain.

The poor pear, it's still all the rage to hate on this tree.

The backlash began when those first clones approached the end of their short, stunted lives. They began to reveal key glitches in their system, most notably the inability to grow strong crotches between the trunk and the main branches of the canopy, what's called the *scaffold branches*. Hanging together by the weakest of wood, the old pears started to crack up and fall apart, right there on the streets too, a pitiful sight. Things were even worse below the pavement. Unaccustomed to growing in such compacted soil and tight quarters, what's called a *tree pit*, the roots didn't have enough room to support their over-extended, overgrown, mutant bodies.

For short-term use, it may be acceptable, wrote Michael Dirr in his Encyclopedia of Trees and Shrubs, *but to plant entire streets with this cultivar is playing biological Russian roulette*. On his blog, he called it a *disaster* and recommended that it be phased out of production.

But of course no one was listening.

Every time a clone went down, the government was there to offer another one for the pit, the latest versions from the experimental farms. Eventually the private sector nurseries got into the game, breeding their own cultivars from the government stock. Competition between the nurseries and the government helped keep the inventory high and the prices down, irresistible bait for anybody tasked to purchase ornamental trees on a budget for the Streets Departments, Parks Departments, strip malls, corporate complexes, and housing developments.

They meant well, I suppose. They certainly did their best to assure us that each new model corrected one of the structural flaws from the previous pear, just take your pick. Take the new ones with wider and stronger scaffold branching, makes your street furniture less susceptible to wind and ice damage. And make sure you check out the autumn blaze or the aristocrat model, what with the more dominant trunk, or the cleveland select, or the whitehouse, or the latest version of the bradford or the trinity which was one of the first pears to move away from the egg-shaped crown and towards the more structurally sound pyramidal shape, or go big and get the chanticleer, named Urban Tree of the Year by City Tree Magazine.

The next chapter to this disaster shouldn't come as any surprise.

The clones learned how to replicate on their own. With so many different makes and models out on the town, there was nothing to stop them from cross-pollinating and making new versions of themselves. Together they created a new unstoppable breed of pears, a mongrel ruderal offspring even more tenacious than their wild ancestors. Frank Meyer was right. This tree could grow under any condition: under bridges, in alleyways, in open fields and idle farms, highway shoulders, train tracks, the edges of cemeteries and community gardens, and any day now into our native wood. Even the U.S. Government has completely changed its tune. *Pyrus calleryana* is now considered an official invasive species by the Department of Ag and they were named Weed of the Week by the Forest Service in September 2005, which, also no surprise, was the same year it won Urban Tree of the Year by the Society of Municipal Arborists.

Do not plant callery pear, it says right now all over the government websites.

But, Frank, they're still not listening. They just dropped off four more in my neighborhood, four more callery pears now waiting for me every morning at the 47th Street trolley stop. Got here one morning and there they were, all lined up, one for the Hair Show Barbershop, one for the Jim Roebuck District Office, one hanging out in front of Dahlak Paradise Ethiopian restaurant, and the last one for Lucky Chinese.

Everything else on this corner from the streetlights to the parking meters has been updated and replaced, I guess I should've known the callery pears were next. I'm not exactly sure which varieties we got – is there anybody out there who can really tell them apart – but the trees are already showing signs of duress and starting to crack up. The first tree in line already has a branch so hunched over it takes up its own seat on the new ergonomic bench. To my Squirrel Hill neighbors, consider yourselves warned: these are dangerous companions during moments of wind and rain and especially snow, and somewhere high above us poor trolley riders there's the West Philly widow-maker only one bad storm away from its final swing.

From 47th Street, my trolley ride stops at every corner on its way through University City. There are always new crops of students moving in and out of the neighborhood but I've been riding this same trolley for so many years now I can always find

Callery pear in South Philly;
From the City of Philadelphia.gov: "Arborists from Parks & Recreation
are on-call to respond to tree emergencies;" call 911 for emergencies, 311
for non-emergency requests, and PECO at 1-800-841-4141 if a tree has
fallen on wires.

a few familiar faces inside the crowded car. We exchange smiles and nods and the smallest of small talk. Lately it's been making me feel like I'm just repeating the same day over and over again, riding the same giant loop from sunup to sundown. Sometimes the feeling is so powerful that I can fool myself into thinking it's really yesterday. Or ten years from now. I worry that this will happen so often that I won't be able to stop the cycle.

I feel the evening of life slowly descending upon me, Frank Meyer wrote, *and the fearful sorrow which hangs all over earth does not make life the same it once used to be.*

As we ride down Baltimore Avenue, we drive past even more callery pears. Some of them I've known for years now but we've never exchanged a word. Most of them are the older types and have been in the neighborhood since before I moved here. So are most of the people I recognize on the trolley. They're all bending and breaking in different ways but they all look the same to me. I have the funny feeling the trees feel the same way about us. If so, then here's an observation from a fellow cookie cutter: we aren't the only things in this city mass-produced for the rat race.

Times certainly are sad and mad, Frank Meyer once wrote, *and from a scientific point of view so utterly unnecessary.*

The most notable pear on my ride is the one growing on 43rd Street, second tree in from the corner of Baltimore Ave. It doesn't really look any different from the other callery pears in the neighborhood but that's where Bob Bimmerstock sets up his fruit stand every Saturday morning at the Clark Park farmers' market. He's been setting up under that tree for over 25 years now. According to Bob, that pear's been there the whole time too, the stories you could tell.

I'm not sure why but sometimes I like to imagine Frank Meyer at the farmers' market. I like to picture him waiting in Bob's line with the rest of the shoppers. I feel like he's the only one who would appreciate the scene the way I do, pear tree and pear farmer working together again. Nobody knows who Frank really is but I recognize him right away. The way we smile at each other, he knows his secret identity is safe with me. In the fall, he's just one more Squirrel Hill neighbor, lined up around Bob's tables, shopping under the shade for the bosc, the seckel, two types of anjou and two more varieties from Frank's old haunting grounds, the yoinashi, which translates to good pear, and the hosui, abundant juice.

Every time he leaves the market, he asks me the same question: if you could be a tree, which tree would you be?

It's not an easy question for me to answer. I have a lot of opinions on the subject. Frank, I've still got a lot of big trees and big dreams in mind. On my best days I am mighty like the oak, tall as a tulip poplar, more steadfast than the spruce, friendly like the beech or as tough as a catalpa, but there are days in between when I'm forced to recognize another type of tree. Sometimes it feels like the decision was made a long time ago. I'm just another callery pear. Much like yourself perhaps. He is kind enough to offer me advice, from one good pear to another: keep moving, speak up, discover something new, learn a few more names before it's too late. Trees aren't the only creatures in this city that can disappear right into the infrastructure.

(above) *From USDA National Agricultural Library,
the Frank N. Meyer Collection,
31 March 1917.*

From Meyer's South China Exploration typescript:
    *"Pyrus calleryana. Dwarf wild Calleryana pears,
    only a few feet high, growing in sterile, decomposed
    porphyrious rock on a badly eroded mountain top,
    elevation c.a. 2,000 ft. a.s. This photo certainly illus
    trates the marvellous [sic] drought-resisting capaci
    ties of this wonderful Chinese pear."*

Currently on the PA Dept. of Agriculture website, the
Noxious Weed and Controlled Plant page:
    *"Callery pear, Pyrus calleryana, was added to
    the Pennsylvania noxious weed list in November
    2021. As a noxious weed, Callery pear may no longer
    be distributed, cultivated, or propagated within the
    Commonwealth. Enforcement of the ban on sale and
    distribution of Callery pear will be phased in over
    two years to allow time for nurseries to eliminate it
    from their stock...*

CATALPA

It all began as a normal evening in July, with the skies still bright and blue and the temperatures still hot and muggy from the long summer day. My camping chair was folded up in one hand and my backpack full of local beer and peaches was in the other as I jumped out the door and headed down the street. I was going to be more than an hour early but I was still in a hurry. I was determined to get a good spot in the shade. Those spots tended to go fast and there were already groups of people, just like me, marching down Chester Avenue to The Bowl for opening night of Shakespeare in Clark Park.

I walked down the street doing my best to get ahead of the pack. In the distance I could see the Shakespeare crew gearing up for the big show, setting up the speakers and running wires to the stage. The grass was already beribboned with tarp and blanket. Troupes of actors and troupes of the usual West Philly weirdos were walking under the trees deep in thought wearing medieval costumes and practicing their lines.

Down Chester Avenue, there was a single line of cars double-parked to drop off the kids and the coolers. I crossed the street, wending a path between the trolleys and the traffic. One of my neighbors handed me a playbill as I entered the park. It was only six o'clock, still early for a summer night, but there was already a buzz in the air and long lines at the taco truck and the water ice cart.

The stage was at the bottom of what we called The Bowl and that's exactly what it looked like. It used to be a pond but when they buried Mill Creek back in the 1860s the pond dried up, leaving behind a great big bowl of grass, and a large flat sandy bottom, a perfect setting for comedies and tragedies. Around the rim of The Bowl there remained a few big trees, most notably a giant sycamore and a rare black oak, that looked like they were still bending over their younger reflections in the pond.

I set up my camping chair in the shade of a tulip poplar, feeling lucky that I found such a good spot. I couldn't remember the last time I was so excited for a summer selection. This year they picked my absolute favorite, *Macbeth*.

"As I did stand my watch upon the hill," Macbeth's messenger will say in Act Five, "I looked toward Birnam and, anon, methought, the wood began to move."

It's one of the greatest scenes in all of Shakespeare but it's always left me wondering. Was Malcolm's trick a real strategy back in medieval times? It seemed like such a complicated ruse. Did armies really advance upon an enemy's castle disguised as trees?

And if so, which tree would I be?

I guess I'd like to think of myself as something mighty, like an oak or a spruce, but if you think about it, those kinds of giants wouldn't be able to move with stealth through a battlefield. You're also ruining the element of surprise if everybody thinks they're big trees. There's no way an entire army of oaks could sneak up on a castle. And the more I pondered the subject the more it seemed likely that the soldiers camouflaged as the kings of the forest were probably the easiest targets, and probably the first among the fallen. No, it'd be best to be an understory tree, methinks, something like a dogwood or a crabapple.

That's just when my phone started lighting up with missed calls and text messages.

I looked at all the notifications suspiciously, trying not to look at them at all, but I couldn't ignore the one from Goldberg.

Turn on the news, he'd sent.

I refused to do it. Instead I reached down and hid my phone in the grass. Unbeknownst to Goldberg and whoever else was trying to contact me, I was going to enjoy the rest of this July day without any new news. Whatever was happening out there in the real world could wait until tomorrow, I assured myself. It was only just last week when I realized that there'd be no summer vacation this year, again, and my only consolation to that bleak realization was knowing there were still a few languid evenings left in the season.

This particular languid evening had my name written all over it.

I picked a peach from my backpack and rolled it under my nose. It was still cold from the fridge. I was cooling off myself, fermenting in the shade. Off to the west, up Chester Avenue, the sun was going down slow and golden. The smell of mosquito repellent wasn't too oppressive yet and in a couple of hours I'd be transported back to foggy, filthy, medieval Scotland to watch the rise and fall of King Macbeth.

Not bad, I thought, for a summer night even if the world, like my phone, was blowing up.

It was Goldberg again: *Dude, wake up and check the news.*

It turned out my day was only just beginning.

I wrote back to Goldberg, *Keep your pants on*, and then I turned on the Action News app. It wasn't hard to find the story.

"Abandoned House Forcing Neighbors To Move Out," the headline rang. "A bad situation is getting worse for a Feltonville family. Problems with a boarded-up house next door are forcing them to pick up and move."

Good, Goldberg sent. *You're awake*.

"This is the problem," the story continued, "a tree is growing from inside the crumbling house next door on West Thelma Street."

I took a deep sigh and accepted the inevitable. I dropped the peach back into the bag, folded up my camping chair, and started climbing out of The Bowl. As soon as I stood up and walked away, two couples started fighting over my spot in the shade. I sent a text message to Goldberg, *I saw the story*, just as this woman stood up in my path and coated herself with aerosol mosquito spray. A big horrible waft of it landed in my mouth, the first thing I'd eaten since lunch.

I could've really used that summer vacation.

Send me photos when you get there, Goldberg wrote back.

The sidewalks were crowded and I was the only one walking away from the park, so it was a lot of pushing and shoving. I scrolled through the rest of my messages as I conquered the crowd. Every message was about this Feltonville situation, about this boarded-up house on Thelma Street being taken over by a tree.

As I was getting into my car, Goldberg was sending me another message: *Where is Feltonville?*

I didn't really know where it was. I just kind of knew it was North Philly, along the Roosevelt Boulevard but right before the Roosevelt Boulevard reaches the Tacony Creek, so North Philly, not what we call the Northeast. I've never heard much about it. As far as I could remember, this was the first time that news from Feltonville had ever reached my outpost in West Philly and I didn't know anyone, friend or foe, who lived anywhere near Feltonville.

It's inside North Philly, I sent to Goldberg, *on the border of the Tacony Creek watershed.*

I looked it up on my phone to figure out a route. On the map it looked like one of the smallest neighborhoods in the entire city, so small that it was combined with Juniata. That's how it was labeled on the map: Juniata Park/Feltonville.

I dug deeper online and started scrolling through the official city data, which revealed this shocking statistic: 28,000 people crammed into 1.2 square miles. That was more than double the average for the whole city. Did I really want to go to such a dense part of town? Each household also had 1.4 cars so parking was going to be dense too. A closer look at the data revealed a neighborhood rich with diversity. It looked like people from all over the world landed in Feltonville: Puerto Rico, Trinidad, Jamaica, Mexico, Korea, Cambodia, significant populations for all, with an estimated 27 languages spoken in the homes and on the streets.

Goddamn, I thought, I don't think I could even name 27 languages.

I buckled up. Based on the map Feltonville looked like it was easy to miss. The way I'd be approaching, I figured it'd be best to hop off the Boulevard at Hunting Park, which meant taking the Wingohocking Street exit and wending my way from there, knowing if I hit Hurley Street then I went too far.

I put the car into gear and took off, with the funny feeling that none of those names meant anything to anybody who didn't live a stone's throw away from Feltonville.

I've never heard of it, Goldberg replied.

I drove through my neighborhood to the highway entrance and slid right into place in the usual interstate traffic. We moved down the highway together in spurts, one long crowded conveyor belt. Eight miles later I merged into the chaos that is the Roosevelt Boulevard. It's one of the biggest roads in Philadelphia, twelve lanes across at certain points. It's also one of the most dangerous rides in the entire East Coast megalopolis, two of its intersections ranking in the top three riskiest intersections in the country, according to State Farm Insurance.

I drove down it on high alert, one eye on the map and both hands on the wheel, and I still missed the turn for Feltonville. I flew right by it, unable to separate myself from the pack and get into the right lane. According to my phone, now I had to start looking for something called the C Street exit.

That's crazy, I thought. I didn't even know the city had a C Street but there it was on my phone, right in order between B and D.

I turned down it. At every stop sign I was going deeper and deeper into undiscovered country, cruising through Philly's Alphabet City and entering Feltonville east of the sun, west of the moon. For the first few blocks of the neighborhood it was all suburban living and the only thing to see were houses, what looked like the same house actually, on repeat from corner to corner. Even the slight variations in the model repeated themselves from block to block. The flora suffered from the same lack of diversity. Feltonville was basically a monoculture when it came to trees: sycamore, ginkgo, sycamore, ginkgo with the occasional pear or cherry to break up the monotony.

I wrote back to Goldberg: *Doesn't look like Feltonville has much to say.*

According to the map, Thelma Street was coming up around the corner from the intersection of Wyoming and Rising Sun. I pulled into the first spot I could find, right in front of a tight row of retail stores: the Real & Tasty Carribbean Food take-out window, the 10 to 10 Nail Salon (it hit me later that day when I returned to my car that *10 to 10* meant it was open from 10am to 10pm), a cell phone store, an auto-tag store, a signmaker store, and an El Spanish cafe on the cater-corner.

Getting out of the car, I stepped back into the mugginess that takes over the Philadelphia summer. It was even hotter in this part of town. I turned my back to the sun and leaned against my car. I could feel the hot day sinking behind the rooftops but it was still flooding the whole neighborhood with a blinding glare, this dog day of July about to end with one long, slow sizzle.

I felt into my backpack. The beer and the peaches were still cold, thanks be the gods for their mercy, and I slung the pack over my shoulder and walked towards the intersection.

Halfway there I had to veer into the street because of a truck and van parked on the sidewalk. I guess that's one way to solve the parking problems, I thought. It was funny to me how natural it seemed here in Feltonville, to fill up the sidewalks with cars and vans, and yet that kind of civil disobedience would've never flied in my neighborhood.

I waited my turn at the next stop sign and crossed Luray Street with a gang of moms and their strollers. They were paying absolutely no attention to me. I might as well have been the stop sign. Up ahead on the next corner, I could see another auto tag store and the Rodriguez Mini-Mart. In front of that auto tag store the street sign for Thelma was hovering in the air and rippling in the heat waves like a flag.

I was excited to finally see my destination but I aimed instead for the back wall of that mini-mart. I wanted to approach Thelma Street carefully, intentionally, and I saw that back wall as the perfect place to cool off, catch a breath, and quench my thirst.

I slithered into the shade under the awning and popped open a beer. I did it like it was a normal thing for me to do but, as thirsty as I was, I had to admit I had a sudden pang of guilt being on an unfamiliar street with an open container of alcohol in my hand. This was technically a crime: drinking in public, disorderly conduct, vagrancy, nonviolent resistance without a permit. At the very least I deserved a ticket but then again it was technically worth a ticket back in Clark Park too.

Now how come, I asked myself, if I was still at Clark Park, despite being surrounded by families and children, I would've had zero doubts or second thoughts about drinking and rebelling in plain sight.

When I thought about it that way I realized I only felt guilty on account of geography and so, with a cleaner conscience, I leaned into the shade from the mini-mart and enjoyed the rest of the beer with my new friend, the dumpster.

As far as I was concerned it was Shakespeare in the Park all over the city tonight

Looking across the street, I spied one of the few wild trees in the neighborhood. It was growing out of a pile of dirt behind the auto tag store, tall enough to bend over the fence. I squinted through the haze to identify its leaves but a glimpse at the ground quickly solved the mystery. It was an apple tree, and not a crabapple tree either but a real apple. Dozens of apples were scattered on the ground rolling along the curb. Some were bright green and looked hard as rocks. The others were brown and mushy and swarming with yellow jackets.

On the patio with me, behind the dumpster, was another wild tree, this time a mulberry. I wasn't so surprised with that identification. Mulberries are common to this growing zone, and pretty prevalent in the Philly woods especially along the creeks and inside the swamps of Tinicum. They feed herds of local wildlife but for a typical citybilly like me the mulberry was more frequently found like this, as an inner city weed tree. In these kinds of situations it's often referred to as a *trash tree*. All the purple berry juice stains splattered around the patio were the exact reason why the mulberry earned that nickname.

I took another long cool drink. An apple and a mulberry, I thought, two familiar trees and yet this time something was strange about them. Even though I recognized them instantly, I still felt like I was forgetting something about them, something that would prove useful to this quest if I could only remember, like an ancient rhyme that speaks about traveling through a land of apples and mulberries. A land of suspicious fruit. Trash trees among the ornamental gallery. This little corner hideout suddenly felt like a sinister place, festering with wildness despite the facade of civilization, the temple of Chaos behind the minimart. Adding to the mystery, I suddenly felt a draft of a breeze, even more humid than the surrounding air, coming from behind the mulberry.

When I bent back the branches I revealed a hidden narrow alleyway.

"Well, I'll be," I spoke into the beer bottle.

And by alleyway I really meant a trench, tunneling behind the houses on Thelma. It was hard to see exactly what was down this narrow way but it looked like it was used for the people on Thelma to store their trash cans, or maybe it was only for emergencies like a fire escape.

I knew, reluctantly, that this would have to be my path. According to the news stories, I was supposed to be looking for a boarded-up house and for some reason inherently found in places like Feltonville it was going to feel a lot less shady sneaking through a back alley than straight up approaching a boarded-up house.

The craziest part about it was how green the alleyway was, all overgrown with ivy and weeds and grasses. I clawed my way through them as I stomped down the trench. There was a stink to the atmosphere, that smell of human waste and plant rot, the urban pickling process working hard here, and every few feet I stepped on some sort of plastic bag that ended up disturbing a frenzy of flies, green-eyed buggers that flew around my ankles and up my shorts. I'd just stumbled into a real concrete jungle.

As I passed behind each house, I peered through the fences into the backyards and patios. I was on the lookout for boarded-up windows or doors, for any signs of long neglect, or for any glimpse of the tree itself. I was nervous about finding other faces looking back at me. It was not a good idea to go around Feltonville startling people. But lucky for me all the backyards were empty, minus some clutter, and every window was dark and tenantless.

I'd just discovered the least populated street in all of Feltonville.

Ahead of me, something rustled inside a thicket of tall grass. For one wild second I thought it was the tree itself, snaking into the trench, unafraid to meet me on the path, but as I stepped closer a seagull burst from the weeds, bounced down the trail and at the first shaft of sunlight flew into the sky.

More seagulls, previously hidden, burst from the weeds and joined the escape.

"Everybody settle down," I said. "I come in peace."

I watched the flock of birds fly into the blinding sun. As I lowered my eyes, I spotted a splash of leaves growing from the next rooftop.

As I walked deeper down the trench, I spied a slender brown branch hanging off the roof and running like a gutter down the brick wall towards a boarded-up upstairs window.

Jackpot.

The bottom half of the house was covered with vines. You could barely see the bricks and siding underneath. Leaving the trench and entering the back patio area, I had to step over a few metal poles to get closer to the building, relics of a former fence. Above my head the ivy was a thick, shaggy carpet twirling around the utility wires. I entered its dappled shade, breathing in the honeysuckle.

Straight ahead of me, to my delight, there was a knot of wood growing, like a giant pimple, through the brick wall. Clusters of thin branches were shooting out of it. The branches were green and young and weak, easy to snap in half, but they were full of leaves, huge leaves, bigger than my head, dark green and heart-shaped. They were warm to the touch and they left a sticky whitish film on my fingertips.

I took a photo of the leaves and sent it to Goldberg.

This was another familiar tree. Off the top of my head, it probably has one of the highest populations in the entire city. I certainly see them everywhere. I knew its name the moment I saw those huge heart-shaped leaves.

"Catalpa," I said.

Along with the ailanthus and the paulownia, this tree completed the unholy trinity of the most ubiquitous, persistent, tenacious, hardy as hell Philadelphia weed trees.

Could be a catalpa or a paulownia, Goldberg wrote back.

That's a mistake in identification that happens often, I bet, especially when only looking at the tree through a screen. Paulownias also have large heart-shaped leaves but their leaves grow in pairs. The catalpa leaves are usually found in whorls of three. Also, catalpa leaves typically end in a sharper point.

If there's still some confusion, then there's an even easier distinction to find between the two. Look for a fruit. Paulownias have a unique fruit for this area, woody almond-shaped capsules. The catalpa fruit is completely different, a slender pod of beans. I couldn't find any bean pods hanging from the branches coming out of the wall but they must've been growing from the part of the tree on the roof because the backyard was littered with them.

I picked one up. It was very thin, the width of a green bean, and very long, at least a foot long. It was also completely dried out, with a penny-colored shade of brown and a papery texture. There was a weightlessness to it. The name *catalpa* comes straight from the language of the Creeks who lived in Georgia, so sometimes you'll see the tree spelled out as *catawba* and, thanks to these long brown beans it has a few other colloquial names.

"Indian cigar tree," I said.

I snapped another photo and sent it to Goldberg and then I dropped the pod on the ground with the rest of the beans.

Definitely a catalpa, Goldberg wrote back. *Try to get closer.*

But that was not an easy feat. I had to duck under its thick canopy of leaves and, holding my backpack in front of my face like a shield, I burrowed my way through its brush. When I finally reached the house I was all flipped around. My back slammed against the brick wall and, gasping for air, I slid down the wall into a crouch.

The knot of wood was just off to my left. I turned to face it like it was sitting next to me on the trolley.

"I read about you on the nightly news," I said.

I leaned back and sent another photo to Goldberg. Then I put the phone on the ground and began my investigation. I put my hand underneath it to guess its weight. Rock solid. Dry as a bone. And I could feel a rippling pattern in its grain. Closer to the wall, there were shards of cement and red dust

embedded in its wood. It was hard to tell where the catalpa began and the house ended.

It's tearing the house apart, Goldberg wrote. *Look for its roots.*

But that was the thing. I couldn't find any roots. I kicked around the green and yellow leaves piled up next to the house but not one little bump of a root. Just more bricks and beans. I couldn't see how it was connected to the ground, how it was growing out of the soil.

I'd never met anything like it before. The catalpa was just sort of hanging off the roof and oozing out of the wall.

"C'mon, catalpa," I said. "Where's the rest of you?"

I looked up and lined myself up so I was standing underneath the splash of leaves on the roof. I reached out to touch the wall in front of me. Even before my fingers touched the ivy, I could tell

there were no bricks underneath.

"Found you," I said.

I dug both of my hands into the vines and pulled them back. It made a ripping sound as I peeled it away from the wall. Some bricks got stuck in the tendrils of vines and dangled in mid-air. Some bricks fell to the ground and shattered against the bricks already there. The ruckus echoed down the trench alerting Feltonville. That old feeling of guilt and shame creeped back into my heart as I stared into the hole in the brick wall that I just uncovered, as I stepped closer to examine the thick, naked branch that I just exposed.

I snapped a photo of the branch and sent it to Goldberg.

Or maybe this was the trunk.

Whatever it was, it was broad and round, shaped like a wide pipe. I tried to remember what I knew about catalpa bark but the

only thing I recalled was that it wasn't distinctive at all. It was the usual rough, thick, dark gray platelets. That's what made this part of the tree so weird. This surface was smooth, thin, damp and dark brown, more crust than bark.

I reached out to touch it but some inner apprehension halted my hand right above its surface, where luminescent follicles of cilia suddenly stood at attention and grazed my palm with a light tickle.

And then I finally got it. This was neither the branch nor the trunk.

Goldberg's next message confirmed it: *That's the root.*

I cracked open another beer and kept my eyes on this strange tree. I couldn't tell if it was staring back but I had my suspicions. It did feel like someone was watching me. Maybe it was the neighbors finally catching on and, if that were true, then who could blame them for keeping their eyes on this pair of Feltonville scofflaws, one of them breaking the rules of the natural world, the other one bending the rules of society, both of them guilty of trespassing.

Can you tell where it begins? Goldberg wrote.

I guess it all began with a bean. I looked up to that little splash of leaves. I tried to imagine the landscape on that roof. I pictured small piles of leaves turning to humus, compost between the shingles, birds' nests in the cracks of the chimney, gutters full of earth. If you happen to be born a seed, all you really need in this world is a sunny, damp, dirty place to land.

That roof would do.

Looks like it starts on the roof, I wrote back.

Once you've got a roof under your feet and a place to call home, I guess the next step would be to sprout. From what I hear, that's the most vulnerable stage. Out in the wilds it's all too easy for the canopy to overshadow something as delicate as a sprout. And you can't expect any of the other trees to bend out of the way for you either. You got to find your own path to the sky. And even if you get lucky, even if you're able to find one little sunbeam to call your own, at any moment you can get eaten by a mouse, a deer, a turtle, or stepped on by some larger mammal. It's a hard-knock way of life but I guess that's why they call it a jungle.

When you think of it that way, a Feltonville roof wasn't so bad.

Where does it go from there? Goldberg sent.

From there you've got to build the parts of a tree. You grow a leaf to catch the light and you start making your own food. You store the sugar to build the heartwood. With wood comes stability, a sense of permanence, the beginning of a foundation. As you get older, you try your best to flower with the hope that the flower, in this case, will one day be a bean. For that to happen you need to be attractive to bees. One of the first priorities would be a consistent source of water. No tree, not even a catalpa, was going to get very far without some sort of well. That shouldn't be too hard to find in a vacant house. Myself, I'd head straight for a leaky pipe. Once you figure out the water situation, you lay down a root.

From there it's just survival, I wrote back.

It can't be easy being a tree in this city, whether you're a magnificent specimen like an oak or spruce or you're a weedy little bastard like the catalpa. Any given day could be your last. Somewhere nearby there's an ax with your name on it, a highway or a wire headed in your direction, a bolt of lightning destined to strike you down, or another tree, a faster tree, ready to take your spot. Right place, wrong time. Or you just peter out, your well runs dry, a little more year after year, and before you know it you're parched and petrified, fodder for insects, or swept away like dust by a strong wind. You've got to be a lot lucky and you've got to be a little graceful but perhaps it's better to be like the catalpa. Tenacious. Persistent. Invasive.

Be a catalpa and at least you've got a fighting chance.

"But, catalpa," I said, "you won't win."

I believed that when I said it but, it turns out, it was even truer than I thought because, five years later, I found myself driving past Feltonville again and I took a quick detour to see for myself whatever happened to that catalpa. This time I walked down Thelma in the middle of the street and approached the house from the front. Or I would've approached the house if it was still there. Instead, there was a gap in the row homes. The house numbers skipped from 165 to 169. The boarded-up house was completely gone. The tree was gone too and the void where both house and tree once lived was now being used as a driveway for three cars, although it really only had room for two.

But maybe that's how something like a city falls to the wilds. One tree, one house at a time. The first wave of attack could be happening right now, the enemy already inside the gate. The weed trees are already squatting in the bush, getting stronger. Maybe Malcolm had the right idea. The way the wilds advance. The way the wood moves. How it storms the brick and steel castle.

And, if so, which side would I be on?

I put the empty bottle back in my bag. The night sky was descending upon the city in dark ribbons. The seagulls were returning to roost. I could hear them landing in the trench, ruffling the grass into nests. The large heart-shaped leaves began to droop, finishing a full day's work under the Strong Sun Moon and settling in for the short night.

I was getting ready to call it a day myself.

I stepped forward and grabbed the ends of the sheet of ivy and flattened it back against the wall with the rest of the vines. The tendrils seemed to lock hands right away, the curtain back on the window, the catalpa the secret king in waiting once again.

You cannot stop the wilds, Goldberg sent.

I smiled and headed back down the trench. I always liked it when Goldberg quoted me.

Back in the day, Goldberg could hold his own against any other tree-hunter here in the city and, for a while, we were known as somewhat of a team, partners in crime you might say, but he turned homesteader years ago. He was a country mouse now, moved to the suburbs with the wife and kids, had to buy a lawnmower and a weed whacker, and he was real proud of the ornamental dogwood growing in his yard.

I don't see the catalpa too much anymore, Goldberg wrote.

No, I bet he didn't. You don't find a catalpa barbecuing on the back deck.

I can't say I miss it very much, he sent.

I'm pretty sure I would. The catalpa was a dirty player, no doubt, but you had to give it some respect. Each one of the prominent Philly weed trees have their own individualized attributes, and their own specialized tactics to invade different parts of the infrastructure, but the catalpa was definitely one of the best at turning cement into a garden, bricks into soil.

It didn't start out that way. The catalpa's original native range was limited to the southern states, where it enjoys a somewhat better reputation. It also has one or two interesting facts in its natural history. In the 1800s, railroad tycoons would plant groves of them ahead of construction, a quick source of wood as the train tracks reached further west. It was introduced to Philly as an ornamental, prized for its orchid-like flowers and its hardiness as a street tree, but it didn't take long for the catalpa to escape into the grid and find its own niche in the Philadelphia understory. It happened fast too, like the catalpa couldn't wait to bust out and get free. In no time at all, it went from the arboretums to the alleyways, from the parks to the potholes. This city can do that to you sometimes.

Portrait of Johannes Kelpius by Dr. Christopher DeWitt, 1705.

CAVE OF KELPIUS

Painful Kelpius from his hermit den
By Wissahickon, maddest of men...
-- Charles Greenleaf Whittier

Once he was in charge of the charter and in place as governor, William Penn began promoting the Pennsylvania colony to the people back home. He did his best to make the colony sound like a place of abundant resources and liberties, with everyone full on fish and fowl. Two years into the project, he wrote what would become his most famous attempt to solicit more adventurers and purchasers. It was entitled "Letter to the Free Society of Traders," sometimes referred to as "An Advertisement for Colonists."

The air is sweet and clear, he wrote, *the heavens serene, like the south parts of France, rarely overcast*. The advertisement goes on to describe in detail the land, the rules, the waters which were *generally good*, the flora, the fauna, the crops both natural and artificial, and the Natives, *the most merry creatures that live*. It's a picturesque vision of Philly – *the woods are adorned with lovely flowers* – and he makes the young city sound like such a beacon of goodness. Everybody is welcome, he was saying to the world, and you know he meant it, but I bet even Penn was freaked out when Kelpius and his band of forty mystics arrived to his new city.

This would be 1694, twelve years after Penn's own landing. By then the Philadelphia docks would've already welcomed the first Mennonites, the first Catholics, the first Jews, and fellow Quakers from all over Europe but Philly hadn't seen anything like Johannes Kelpius before.

He was originally from Transylvania, from the same birthplace as Vlad the Impaler. During his university days, he became attracted to a group called the Chapter of Perfection, led by a renegade priest named Zimmerman, an outcast from the Church for his new age ideas and ambition. Zimmerman died in 1693 and Kelpius the star pupil took command of the flock. They sailed towards Penn's promise and settled first in the Germantown neighborhood. A short time later, they ventured into the woods of the Wissahickon gorge. They cleared out enough room for a hermitage and built a tabernacle among the trees. They lived outside in primitive shelters, studied medicine and alchemy, played their music, mapped the stars, and predicted the futures.

Make a new heart in me, Kelpius wrote in one of his hymns. *I shall be scorned by fools.*

He was actually the subject of one of the colony's first oil paintings, which would've been a rare opportunity to get a sense of the real man behind the legend, so too bad the painting lacks any meaningful details. And the dimensions are all out of whack too. For example, it's hard to tell if his book is lying on top of the desk or floating in mid-air. And the desk has only one leg, maybe two, another thing that's hard to tell. Kelpius is sitting in a wooden chair facing the painter. He's wearing a long blue robe, a colonial Snuggie. His face is strange and pointed, void of any distinctive features, one grade above a stick figure face:

black eyes, thin smile, chin and cheeks smooth and hairless. Is he completely hairless? Only 26 years old and it looks like he's completely bald under his giant yarmulke. And then the weirdest part of the entire painting is his gesture. His right hand is bent across his lap, clutching the left arm of the chair, and his other hand is raised to his face pointing to his left temple. He's either massaging a headache or trying to read my mind.

By all accounts, his flock stayed at forty monks, their original size. I am guessing, unlike his master Zimmerman, Kelpius wasn't interested in recruiting new hermits. Or perhaps he just wasn't good at it. When it comes to his actual prophecies, it's difficult to know for certain what he was even trying to say. The parts that I think I understand have a lot of complicated math and it was all reliant on poor measurements of the stars and planets anyway. By far, its biggest glitch was the urgency. According to Kelpius's calculations the world was supposed to end that year, 1694, something to do with a verse in the Book of Revelations: *an enormous red dragon with seven heads and ten thorns and seven crowns on its heads; its tail swept a third of the stars out of the sky...the woman fled into the wilderness to a place prepared for her by God.*

That was a tough sell to the people living in Philadelphia at the time and, really, what's the big deal about the end of the world anyway? Most of the people I know have a doomsday once a week in this city.

Kelpius was a believer though. He spent forty days and forty nights of 1694 living in a cave in the Wissahickon woods. After the calendar flipped uneventfully to 1695, he still kept to the Wissahickon. The other millenarians were more inclined to venture forth into the city. They became known as the Hermits of the Wissahickon, or the Mad Monks of the Ridge, or sometimes The Society of the Woman in the Wilderness.

His cave still survives. It's located at the intersection of two trails, in between the East Falls and Manayunk neighborhoods, high upon the steep spine of bedrock that runs from the Henry Avenue Bridge to Ridge Avenue. Looking down the gorge, two hundred feet below, the Wissahickon Creek and Lincoln Drive flow towards Center City.

Deep in the woods, as the Kelpius poem goes, *where the small river slid.*

Let's get the technicality out in the open now: this is not really a cave. It's a springhouse, a common feature of a colonial homestead, usually the size of a single room, built over a spring or dug into a hill, fortified with bricks and locked with a gate. It was like an outdoor refrigerator, with the constant cooling temperatures of the spring water protecting the meat, the veggies, the dairy, and the hermit from spoiling. Kelpius's springhouse is near the site of the original tabernacle. It's carved right into the steep slope of the woods.

In front of its entrance the ground is cleared of any big trees but the rest of the woods has grown and flourished all around it. In springtime it's surrounded by yellow celandine and snowdrops. In the fall, the trails are slippery with red and yellow leaves. When winter comes the only sound is the drumbeat of the bamboo grove somewhere nearby. I've never been able to find it.

During every season the entrance to the springhouse looks the same: a black screen of pure darkness, a shadowy doorway. I have to lower my head to clear the threshold and enter the darkness. Once inside I have to keep my neck in my chest or stoop down to my knees in order to fit comfortably. It's a small space, less than eight paces long, less than five wide, but when I turn around, the entrance looks far away, a distance that seems to grow the longer I stare through the window of the world. Stay long enough and I sometimes get the funny feeling that I'm stuck inside the belly of a beast but the beast is a planet.

That's a cave to me.

Kelpius lived in the Wissahickon until his death in 1708 at age forty-one. Some sources say he was 35 when he died. *He was of frail constitution*, one of his biographers wrote, *which soon broke down after frugal fare and abstemious habits and the extremes of our variable climates.*

The other monks buried him in the woods, whereabouts unknown, and then, one by one throughout the years, most of them left the woods and blended into higher society. Research shows the pessimists contributing to the city as school teachers, court criers, clock makers, bookbinders, and organists. Only six monks stayed in the Wissahickon and stayed true to the order, each one withdrawn to their own cabin in the woods. Sightings of them appear in different accounts, mostly from the millers working down by the river. They reported on occasion the sight of monks marching single-file across the ridge. The last one died in 1765 and was buried with the others in a small Germantown graveyard on High Street. The cemetery measured 40 feet by 40 feet and was known in the neighborhood as Spook Hill until parts of St Michael's Church was built on top of it, 1859.

It is said that the woods near Kelpius's cave is haunted, and that's true, but only in the sense that every woods is a haunt, a place to visit habitually and to inhabit only on occasion. This could be where Kelpius went wrong. He turned the woods from a haunt into a home and then, his fatal flaw, he became a homebody.

From what I've read, you can't flip it around like that. Our proper role is the visitor, our Tarot Card the Guest, and the first etiquette for any guest: never overstay your welcome. No matter how much we enjoy the visit. No matter how much we feel at home. There's so much going on in his woods. The trees and the mountains are constantly walking, either climbing to the top of the ridge or falling over into the gorge. The wind blows the flowers into the sunlight. I try to shoo away the bugs around my head and high above acorns fall off the branch and land near my feet. There are so many birds on the wing, so many mushrooms on the stump, too many trees to name, and yet at the end of every visit we're the ones withdrawing from all these fellow earthlings.

Who's the hermit now?

Into whatever land I come, he wrote, *I come into my own.*

Somewhere in every woods there is a threshold that's not meant to be crossed, a ridge too dangerous to climb. Yonder side can turn a scholar into a bushman, a believer into a heretic, the springhouse becomes a cave, the loner becomes a hermit. But life on the safer side has its price too. We'll never belong here, our membership revoked many moons ago. We can go in but then we have to go out, the whole time scaring away the wildlife. Why do they always run away? It's because these woods are haunted, terrorized the moment we pass under its shade. Like the old Gothic tales, that's the twist. We're the haunters, not the haunted. And stay too long, like Kelpius, way past the curfew of the civilized mind, and a choice will eventually reveal itself among the trees and stones. Go home or go native.

Kelpius chose the cave.

There are three ways to get there. The longest route begins by parking near the apartments on Sumac Street, walking to the end of the road, and finding the tight trailhead next to the utility pole. On this path the understory steals the show, multi-flora rose and rhododendron growing from dogwood to dogwood, the cherries here have black trunks, and the entire trail bends around the giant footholds of the tulip poplars, tallest trees of the land. Perhaps most abundant is the winged euonymus that creeps right up to the trail. It's a common shrub popular for its autumn blaze, a fire-engine red that gives the plant its colloquial name of *burning bush*, but that's a reference to another epic, a different kind of wilderness prophet tale.

The most strenuous path begins at the bottom of the woods, starting on the bike trail on Lincoln Drive. Look for the Help Locator 100 sign for a good place to begin the climb. Best to get a running start. This way is a steep dash up the gorge. Which of these big trees were here during Kelpius's time? Which top of which tree was brushed by the hem of Kelpius's robe when it was but a sapling growing through the rocks? On the climb, the roots of the hemlock trees are used for stairs.

I prefer to approach the cave from downhill. This way the journey starts in the car with a sharp turn off Henry Avenue and a poetic parking spot among the houses on Hermit Lane. At the end of Hermit Lane I can jump onto the Yellow Trail, perhaps the longest trail in the entire Wissahickon. I'm only on it for a little while before I have to veer off and take a smaller path. Look for the wooden pole and make the turn. And stay alert. Right from the start this side-trail is narrow and crooked, a lot of dips and plunges, a lot of switchbacks in both directions, then a

meandering tour through a grove of beeches followed by a steady rise towards the springhouse. It's a devious path too. Sometimes the pit of the gorge is only a misstep away. Sometimes it feels like I'm walking in circles, all told a serpentine puzzle of a path, as it should be, that completes the circuit from Hermit Lane to the cave of Kelpius and his doomsday dale.

At the beginning of the Yellow Trail, someone has scratched into the park bench: *the hermit is watching*. Or it could be *walking*. It's hard to tell.

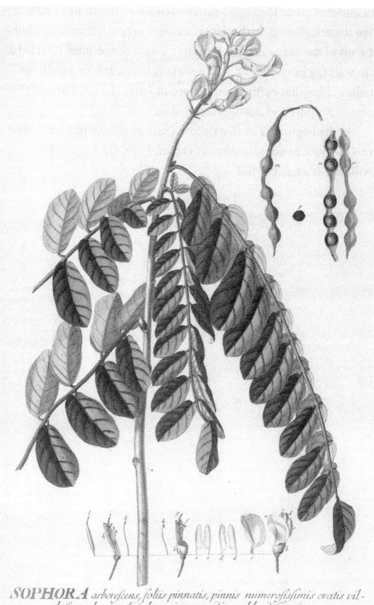

SOPHORA arborescens, foliis pinnatis, pinnis numerosissimis ovatis villosis, caule simplici, leguminum nodis valde distinctis.

a. flos integer; b. calyx. c. vexillum. d. ambae alæ. e. ambæ carinæ foemineæ. f. stamina et a germen calyci. h. ichni inclusio. b. imum stamina et i. germen a calyce nudata. k. l. stamina longe breviora, seperatum. l. germen in stylo brevi et stigmate obtuso; m. legumen maturum. n. dol. retra altera ablata, cujusmodi denudatio. o. valva ablata a facie interna; p. semen.

Illustration by German botanist and entomologist
Georg Dionysius Ehret (1708 - 1770).

CHINESE SCHOLAR TREE

It was introduced to Europe in the 1750s as a member of the necklacepod family with the common name of *pagoda tree*. It received the binomial nomenclature of *Sophora japonica* from the great Professor Linnaeus himself and was soon regarded by the European botanists as a courtly, upright, shimmery tree from the East. About a hundred years later, a cloud of suspicion began following it around. Rumors suddenly swirled that it'd been traveling under the wrong name all those years, just as the tree started making a similar reputation here on the other side of the ocean among the Turtle Island gardeners.

The taxonomists rushed back to the libraries to correct the error and update the field guides. They moved the tree to a much smaller genus, still within the pea family, and bestowed upon it the more multiloquous name of *Styphnolobium japonicum*. In some circles of society, it kept the name *pagoda* or *necklacepod*. Sometimes you still see it referred to as *Sophora*. I happened to make its acquaintance during my university days and although I cannot remember which Latin name our dendrology professor used to introduce it to the class, at one point during his lecture under its shade, he called it the *Chinese scholar tree* and that is the name that has stuck in my mind.

It was a rare tree back then. I can recall only that single specimen growing on the main campus. It was planted further back from the paved paths but its upper boughs had a terrific arch that swooped across the entire lawn almost reaching the sidewalks of College Avenue.

The professor stepped onto the grass and pointed to the lomentaceous fruit right above our heads. By that point in the semester, we'd already observed many examples of the native legumes found in the pea family but these were unlike all the others. These were dangling over us in iridescent shades of green and yellow, neon legumes. Even more exotic, there was a constriction in between each pea, so every pod looked remarkably like a string of greenish-gold pearls, hence the name *necklacepod*.

I remember thinking that it was a very handsome tree. I liked the way its trunk grew out of the ground, so straight and true it seemed to snap to attention. I admired the way it stood in the grass with a vigilant command over the campus. This was a tree that stood on watch. I was not surprised when our professor mentioned that, in its native land, it was often found planted near the entrances of ranger stations and Buddhist temples, hence the name *pagoda tree*.

Then it's as steadfast as it is handsome, I thought.

To my delight I found myself mimicking its posture. I straightened my slouch, sucked in my gut and cast my own slim shadow of a pole. For one wild and vivid daydream we were twin sentries stationed on the same lawn, eyeing each other.

Who goes there, I thought.

It seemed to inch forward the harder I focused. The space between our gaze went as silent as the Void. Suddenly I was alert for any reckless move it might make towards my classmates and our professor.

148

I'm on to you, I said in my head. I see you, tree.

Its reply sounded like a warning: Know your enemy and know thyself, kid.

We walked deeper under its shadow, closer to the trunk. Its pool of shade was big enough to house the entire class. I marveled at the way it seemed to be two trees at once. One tree was planted in the grass like an ascending tower, the other tree floated above us as a cloud of green leaves, raining necklacepods.

I remember thinking: this would be a good life, a consistent life, to watch the seasons turn and the years go by from a single vantage in the grass, to have a station upon this earth, to stand in place but reach so far and dig so deep.

There is only one difference, said the tree, between a groove and a grave.

I lifted my eyes like a crane, staring higher into its leaves and branches.

The depth, I replied.

My eyes traveled the length of its trunk all the way to its summit. Up there, the tree lurched backwards, at the angle of a drawn slingshot, and then it fractured into six large coiling limbs. The limbs formed the roots of its splendid panoramic canopy. The longer I stared at those upper boughs the clearer I understood the construction of that canopy, how each of those limbs split in half, how those subsequent branches split in half again, and then in half again, and again, a division that ran all the way down to the ends of each frivolous twig.

It seemed like the tree had followed a certain pattern in its growth. According to the professor, there were other patterns hidden among the tree, like in the arrangement of its leaves and the timing of its flower, within the texture of its bark and in the structure of its fruit. Each pattern was a distinct characteristic. Become familiar with those characteristics, match all those patterns together, and you can name the tree. That's what the professor was trying to teach us.

To know a fish, said the tree, go to water.

I stepped away from the group and looked around the lawn at the other citizens of the woody kingdom. There was the usual roster of red oaks, honey locusts, and sycamores, the row of cherries, the dogwoods at Murray Hall, the hollies guarding the library doors. Thanks to this class, I was finally able to tell them apart.

I was really getting into it too. Memorizing all the different patterns, looking around the tree for those patterns, it was like cracking a code. Recognizing the way each part of the tree distinguished themselves, the way it led you closer and closer to the name of the tree, it was like reading a treasure map. No wonder a tree identification book, the kinds that were just lists of questions like *are the leaves needle-like or not needle-like* or *is the fruit dry or is it fleshy*, were called *keys*. I wanted to get to the point where I could recite those keys in my head and answer each question with the dart of my eyes. That's the level I wanted to attain in this game.

Plan for what is difficult, said the tree, while it is easy.

I walked around the giant trunk into an even darker, cooler puddle of shade. Without really planning it, I found myself on the opposite side from the class. Thanks to the tree's massive bulk I was hidden now from the other students, and yet the professor's voice was still loud enough to carry over to my side of the trunk.

"The bark is grayish-brown but not that distinct," he said, "although in older trees like this one it does develop these wide flat ridges."

I leaned my back against the trunk until I could feel those flat ridges rubbing against my shoulders.

"And in between those ridges look for these long, deep fissures."

I swayed back and forth across the bark, my shoulders bumping up on those deep fissures in the best way. It made me wonder, and it wouldn't be the last time I wondered, if the tree could feel my touch on its bark or even just sense my presence against its hard and bumpy shell. If I came back here tomorrow and scratched my back against this same spot, would the tree recognize me from today? It crossed my mind then, how difficult it must be for the trees to tell us apart, how impossible to keep track of all the ways we grow, the ways we branch, the timing of our flowers, that confusing habit we all share of never standing still. Where would they look for our patterns? Which ones match us up? Or do we look haphazard to them, indistinguishable, itchy, and rootless? How nice it must be to know how to grow, to be a collection of distinct characteristics, to hear the master dendrologist solve the mystery of your many names.

There are no masters, the tree said, only superior students.

I pressed even harder against the bark. Sounds like something an inferior student would say, I replied.

The professor's voice suddenly moved from my left ear to my right. I could picture him on the other side of the tree, as usual, twirling through the crowd of students as he pointed to different aspects of the tree.

"You probably didn't notice but this tree was flowering when you arrived here for the beginning of the fall term."

He was brilliant, eagle-eyed, a man bored by no twig.

"One of the few trees with such a late summer bloom."

And yet I could not deny that as much as I idolized him, as much as I was inspired by him, there was a side of me that would never be content keeping these identification skills on campus, without any application in the real world. What's the point of only knowing trees on a first-name basis? I wanted these skills to be more than an academic game and I knew I'd never be satisfied stuck in his shoes.

Sometimes I wondered if he didn't feel the same way about his own shoes. On rare moments I was sure I'd caught him standing in the presence of his trees with an air of sadness, a couple times with an unmistakable veil of anger. I can't say those moments ever lasted long but they did have a way of lingering, I thought, in the tremble of his voice, in the frequent sighs, the hints of sarcasm, the way he took off his glasses and breathed on them and rubbed them between the flaps of his untucked dress shirt.

I may have only been a freshman but I was already a superior student when it came to identifying unrequited love.

Wheresoever you go, the tree said, go with all your heart.

"In its native land," the professor said, "those flowers were in bloom at the same time as the annual civil service exams."

I snapped out of the daydream and noticed that the professor was leading the class out of the shade and towards the next tree. I tiptoed around the trunk and rejoined the group as the professor ended his lesson.

"That bloom was an important time of year for the students who graduated that summer. Excellent grades on those exams were key to getting hired by the imperial bureaucracy, hence the name *Chinese scholar tree*."

The following August I did have the fortune to observe those flowers although it would be inaccurate to say that I'd made any special attempt to do so. By that time, I was out of the dorms and living in town and my paths around campus took me past the Chinese scholar several times a week. The flowers were white, tiny, and pretty, not too showy, and the professor was right as rain as usual. Not many trees waited that long into the year to flower. For those two weeks every August the Chinese scholar was the only flowering tree in town.

Every time I hurried by it I had the habit of saying its name either out loud or in my thoughts, but again this didn't make the

Chinese scholar more special than the others. By the end of that summer I'd developed the habit of saying or thinking out loud many of the trees' names as I dragged myself to work, or sulked through campus, or escaped into the woods, or even drove down the highways.

After a few years the trees became landmarks. I'd often find myself uttering their names like it was a necessary procedure to make it safely to my destination, like a turn signal. Other times I would whisper their names in a struggle to ignore whatever, at that particular moment, was troubling my mind, and so their names along my stormy path turned into a solemn, fervent chant. Depending on the magnitude of my troubles this chant sometimes felt like a mantra, at times like a prayer, but more often than not, chanting the trees' names was neither therapeutic nor spiritual. It was, as it should be, a simple etiquette.

I admit: it bothered me that this etiquette went unreciprocated.

I took this habit with me as I left the university and returned to Philadelphia. I was happy to discover that, thanks to the dendrology class, I could identify many of the trees growing along the creeks and rivers, planted on the streets, and living inside the parks. My chant continued, a familiar melody.

As the years passed I noticed the emergence within the city of newer varieties of street trees, unfamiliar to my education and difficult to identify. I was thrilled. My skills, dormant and routine after so many seasons, now sharpened at the sight of strangers in the understory. I dusted off the field guides, back to school once again, back on the hunt, just like old times, only this time I'd be my own teacher.

To my complete surprise, one of the newest and most popular urban ornamentals turned out to be my old friend, the Chinese scholar tree, now one of the most prevalent trees in the entire city.

I couldn't believe it at first. It felt like years since I'd even thought of the Chinese scholar. Every field guide on my shelf still considered them *uncommon*. I certainly hadn't seen a Chinese scholar, nor heard-speak of one, since those university days, and yet suddenly I found myself surrounded by them.

It was a suspicious situation. For many months I still remained unconvinced it was the same tree. I found myself triple-checking every characteristic. I used the slightest variation to put the whole identification in doubt.

My skills must be rusty, I remember thinking, probably misreading the patterns, or maybe my field guides were too old. Maybe some new species of necklacepod had been discovered since their last updates.

Either way I was confused. I was recognizing in these ornamentals all the same characteristics as that namesake from my memories — the single leader of a trunk at the bottom, the multi-branched construction on top, the same bright and

(above and right) *Examples of Styphnolobium japonicum used as a street tree.*

shimmery canopy — but these street trees were so much thinner, and shorter, and less impressive. When planted too close together, they really struggled to put on the pounds. In the fall, it became a common sight to find bean pods that contained only a single pea, a one-pearled necklace. Even worse, not only were they becoming ubiquitous but they looked ubiquitous too, like they all came out of the same Chinese scholar factory.

For that entire year, I didn't care what those field guides were trying to tell me.

Not on my watch, I told them right back, will the great and mighty Chinese scholar turn into an average, upright, boring, admittedly adequate, somewhat handsome, completely ordinary ornamental.

Maybe one day, I told myself, I'll discover that I'd stumbled upon some great forgery, the crime of the century. After all, it did have the reputation for traveling under a mistaken identity.

But, in the end, as always, the keys told no lies. What was once too difficult to accept became too obvious to deny. Looking back, I regret that I wasn't happier to remake its acquaintance but I can't ignore those months of willful uncertainty on my part, nor those genuine moments of disappointment, every time I ran into another one, ran down the keys and ended up in the same spot: *Styphnolobium*, also *Sophora*.

It was during those same moments when I first noticed how dangerously I was leaning towards that same fate.

Things better start turning around fast, I got to thinking, or else I'll be the next one to suddenly show up on the streets in a more diminutive form.

Sometimes I could actually feel myself becoming more ornamental, growing to a more ordinary, less impressive, admittedly adequate collection of patterns. I could never really

pinpoint when it all started, or the location of those first wrong turns, but eventually it became a daily occurrence, the feeling of drifting down, and sinking deeper, into a large and lonely, apparently inescapable, very monotonous stretch of basic existence, what would be labeled, if my life were ever made into a map, as the *doldrums*.

At any moment, I warned myself, that could be me, one more piece of furniture stuck in the cement in some tidy little row like all the other Chinese scholars in this city.

Hence the name *clones*.

It made me wonder, and it made me sad to think about, what paths we both took after those university days, the way those paths separated only to be reunited under these circumstances. How did it happen that both of us had been trained and domesticated into something better suited for these mean streets than those giant lawns of our past. I pictured in my mind the next updates to the field guides. How sad will it read, to go from an average height of seventy feet down to forty, fruits now officially *dull yellow beans* instead of *iridescent necklacepods*. What a letdown, to see creatures once rare and remarkable grow up to be cultivated, locally naturalized, best in zones 4 to 8.

I resisted making the observation for as long as I could but perhaps it was finally time for both of us to face the facts: we were now living in a common world.

It was a conclusion that, once observed, had the habit of riding, uncomfortably, in my train of thoughts as I strolled through the city, or went to work, or even while tramping through the woods. It crossed my paths as often as those street trees. It took on a heaviness that I wasn't used to, like I was carrying it by my side, on my person.

Looking back, a part of me feels like I actually almost made it to the point of no return and the only reason I never made it that far was because of what happened on that one very special, hot and humid, dank and sticky summer day in late August.

That very lucky day when I walked out my front door and bumped into this guy I know named Henry.

He was turning the corner and walking up my street just as I was slamming my front door and descending the porch stairs.

"Hey," he said with a big wave. He hooked his thumbs into the straps of his backpack and headed straight to me.

I tried to reciprocate his friendly smile but I wasn't in the mood to be sociable. Henry was someone I kept running into at random places throughout the city, plus he was a regular at the farmers' market that I managed and a regular at the bars that I liked to hide in. Normally it was a lot of fun to bump into him but lately it was just contributing to the idea that I was stuck on repeat.

No fault of his own but Henry was becoming just another landmark in my doldrums.

"You still into trees?" he asked me.

I sighed. He asked me this every time I bumped into him and my answer never changed. "It's more than just trees, Henry."

"Then what's the kind of tree that's flowering now?"

"Be more specific," I said but I already knew which tree he was talking about. The only reason I didn't answer him right away was because I didn't want to sound too smart or be too short with him.

"Little white tiny flowers," he said, "like in a bouquet."

I walked past him and headed to the corner, gesturing for him to follow my lead.

When we reached the corner I pointed across the street, my nearest Chinese scholar.

"Those white flowers?"

Henry leaned forward and squinted. "Maybe," he said.

"Definitely," I said. "Not many trees have such a late summer bloom."

"But this tree was out in Elmwood, past Bartram Garden."

The Elmwood neighborhood was up around 60th Street, although I wasn't entirely sure about that. Elmwood was uncharted territory for me, a sketchy part of town, not the kind of place known for its trees.

"What were you doing out there?" I asked him.

"That's where my new girlfriend lives."

"Well, it doesn't matter," I said. "It's the same tree. The name is Styphnolobium."

"What?" he said and I repeated it two more times until we both gave up.

"It can't be the same tree," he said.

I shrugged. I walked around him, turning my back to him. I gazed up and down the street hoping for a break in traffic, my first attempt at an awkward exit.

"Was it a street tree?" I asked him.

"Yeah it was but..."

"Then it's the same tree, Henry," I said and waved goodbye. "I got to go."

"...but this tree is like ten times more massive than that thing," he said, pointing to the tree across the street. "This tree I'm talking about has a giant trunk."

I stopped in the middle of the street.

He threw his hands up into the air. "And it's got these amazing branches, high branches."

When I stepped back onto the sidewalk, Henry's arms were still reaching towards the sky, and he was looking into the sky too, like he was staring into the tree that he was trying to describe.

"The branches are huge," he said.

He looked like he was dancing in place.

"They're floating in the sky."

"Henry," I said and I grabbed him by the shoulders. "Where is this tree?" I asked him but he had a dazed look in his eyes. "Come on, Henry. Snap out of it." I clapped my hands in front of his face.

He blinked real hard and recognized me again.

"Henry," I said, "where were you?"

"Hobson Street," he mumbled but I had no idea where that was.

"Come on, I'll drive," I said. "My car is parked around the block."

I walked past him and gestured for him to follow me again. Soon my gait turned into a jog and before I knew it I was running down the sidewalk holding my car keys high above my head.

"68th and Hobson," Henry yelled, already at my heels.

But what he really meant was Hobson and Elmwood. Hobson was one of the narrow streets off Elmwood Avenue between 67th and 68th. Hobson being one-way, I had to drive past it when we arrived. I caught the barest glimpse of the tree as we rode by. Then I missed the turn at 68th, despite Henry's pointing and hollering, so I just pulled over on 70th, no time to waste navigating back through those tight blocks.

We walked from there, down Elmwood Avenue, along the fence-line of the once thriving, now disappearing GE plant, crossed the street at the body shop called Johnny Auto, and ducked down 68th Street. Walking down 68th was a narrow fit, two front doors for every stoop, cars parked on the sidewalk, but halfway down the street the landscape burst open into a large, flat plot of grass known as Buist Park. All of a sudden, it was fresh

160

air and blue skies. Hobson Street was on the opposite side of the park. From that angle, we finally got an unobstructed view of the giant tree.

It was in the middle of the block standing right in between the row homes but it was also soaring, and flowering, above the rooftops. Not even halfway across Buist Park and we were already under its shade.

The road to a friend's house, said the Chinese scholar, is never long.

Information about the tree is now easier to find online but back then it took a good digging through the library and through the archives of the Horticultural Society to piece together the history.

One of the biggest and most mysterious discoveries was a newspaper clipping from the Daily News from 1991. There's no way to tell what the article was about. The only part that survives is the headline which is cut off and reads: **O Today's**

The view down Hobson Street from Elmwood Avenue.

List. Below those words is a list of trees, their addresses, and their ages. That's all that's clipped out. It was paperclipped to a manila envelope that was being stored in a big file cabinet. Five trees down the list there it was: "Chinese scholartree (*sophora japonica*), 2527 S. Hobson Street, 220 years old."

But that last part wasn't true, couldn't be true. That would put the tree back to 1771. This tree wasn't that old. It's from the 1850s, back when that part of West Philly was Robert Buist's enormous 119-acre seed farm and plant nursery called Rosedale, one of the largest and most famous nurseries of its time.

Tutored by Scotland's Royal Gardener, Robert Buist landed in Philadelphia in 1828 at 23 years old. He already had a high reputation for his green thumb. For a brief time he was hired as the Head Gardener for the mansion on top of Lemon Hill, now part of Fairmount Park. After that he managed a block of greenhouses on 13th Street between Lombard and Cedar Streets, Cedar now called South Street. Ever the entrepreneur, he also established a nursery and seed warehouse at 12th and Chestnut. He became famous for his roses, traded seeds and saplings around the world, and is credited for introducing the poinsettia to the United States.

A tree is known for its fruit, said the Chinese scholar, a man by his deeds.

By the 1840s, his business had outgrown the downtown spots so he moved the whole operation to the wide-open plains of future-day Elmwood.

There, he established the legendary Rosedale farm. He began breeding fruit trees for the orchards and ornamental trees for the cities. He wasn't only interested in growing the usual favorites like the planes and elms. He had just as much interest in the more modern ornamentals that were trending in Europe and Asia at the time.

According to the records and archives, this Hobson Street Chinese scholar was the only tree remaining from those nursery days, although knowing that fact never stopped me from searching the Elmwood maze for more Rosedale relics.

Wouldn't it be nice, I thought for the tree, to find more reminders of the old neighborhood, maybe even discover more of the original Chinese scholars living nearby?

I certainly felt nicer, I had to admit, and more invigorated, knowing and visiting the one that was still in town. Unlike college, this time I did make special attempts to visit, although it would be inaccurate to say those visits were peaceful, leisurely activities. They were more like scientific expeditions, or at least it was easier for me to justify those detours if I thought about them that way.

And most of the time it did feel like work, like I went there to study the tree. After all, I would say in my defense, finding this Chinese scholar on the streets of Philadelphia was the equivalent of finding an elephant or a blue whale or a dinosaur.

How you going to stay at home on the couch, I often asked myself, when you know there's a sasquatch on Hobson Street?

There is no such thing, said the Chinese scholar, as an ordinary cat.

In between those visits, I often caught myself wondering how it was doing or what was happening around it. At any moment the tree would surface to the top of my thoughts, unbaited, or appear without

922 Chestnut Street, 1833.

warning as a whisper in the air around me. Once summoned it would spend the rest of the day occupying parts of my mind or on the tip of my tongue. After terrible storms, I would always worry if it was still in good shape, or if it was damaged, or worse, if it would still be there the next time I returned.

I found myself drawn to the tree, again and again, to know the answers to those questions. I was drawn as well to the particular thoughts and daydreams that were frequently called to mind under its shade, as if those thoughts and daydreams had the habit of visiting the Chinese scholar at the same hour as me.

The rain does not fall, said the tree, on one roof alone.

It was never really my goal but, by learning about the tree, I also learned the history of that neighborhood. Driving around and exploring Elmwood, I was thrilled whenever I caught glimpses of that history lingering in the present moment. I was inspired every time I noticed that history haunting the current infrastructure, stamped into the buildings and storefronts, hidden in the

demographics, lost in the matrix of its grid, and written in the names of its streets and parks.

I admired the way the Chinese scholar was a landmark throughout that history. I was sure I could observe, in the bend of its trunk or by the angle of its boughs, the way it had stood watch over the unfolding of those events. I was amazed,

how vigilant and steadfast it was against decades of persistent industrialization, the way it had grown and flourished through the layers of the palimpsest. I also felt rejuvenated, as if this tree's resemblance to the one I knew from the past revived in me a resemblance to my younger self, one who had yet to make so many wrong turns.

The ax forgets, said the Chinese scholar, what the tree remembers.

After a while, I realized that the more time I spent with the tree, the more I was changing the way I regarded all the other Chinese scholars on the streets. I even began to observe, in certain ornamentals, characteristics that couldn't be found in any of my field guides. To my delight these characteristics revealed patterns that went beyond the mechanics of the tree and, to my eyes, seemed to unmask the individual clone's behavior. I know it sounds crazy but I felt like I could observe its personality in the paths of its wooding, in the bends and curves where it must've made an individual choice to grow this way or that. Is that spirit? Is that soul? It was like discovering a brand new key.

Every step, said the Chinese scholar, makes a footprint.

At some point I began making up stories about it.

In one story, Rosedale was in its earliest days. Every tree was still a sapling and this one particular Styphnolobium was the runt of the neighborhood. It had shallow roots or a crooked lean, whatever it was, it was the kind of tree that only got noticed in the ranks when it was failing inspection. Every year, Buist and his nurserymen would walk right on by, an annual reject every time the City came to Rosedale to purchase another harvest of trees.

But look at you now, I'd say in the tale.

Now it was 80 feet tall, by far the biggest Styphnolobium in the City. Looking at it from left to right, it spanned the distance of four row homes, and it really should be five-homes-long but they had to leave a big gap in the middle of the block to give it enough room. It's like the City gave it its own address. And with a circumference of 15½ feet, the City also had to bend the path of the sidewalk around its roots and extend the curb lane so far out into the street you have to drive around it.

In my story, the runt of Rosedale grows up to be so big they had to widen the gutters, skip over houses, foreshorten certain laws, and give up three parking spots just to work around it.

You make a road, said the Chinese scholar, by going down it.

In my other stories I caught it roaming the streets, lending a helping hand or spying on society. It grew so big in my imagination that it became untethered from its spot on Hobson Street and so I let it loose inside the City and inside my mind. I sent it strolling through the neighborhoods like an elder statesman. It kept showing up in the nick of time to fix a flat tire or to thwart a robbery. I would enlist the tree to perform some civic duty like volunteering at the marathon, or donating blood, or appearing before City Council to support the plastic bag ban.

Everywhere we went it seemed to speak from, and on behalf of, the natural world that still survived within the Philly grid.

To my surprise I found myself mimicking its voice inside my head. I found myself impersonating its countenance. I started to evoke its wisdom and adopt its values as I roamed the streets, or showed up to work, when I was heading home or hiking through the woods, as I made my way through the crowded streets and whenever I was able to defy the storms that still crossed my path.

This could be a good life, I remember thinking, a worthy life, to seek out more voices from that natural world. I could tell it was still hiding within the city, still springing up where it could. It wasn't beat, not yet.

Perhaps, I got to thinking, I should reacquaint myself with all the other citizens of the woody kingdom. What if instead of searching for rare and remarkable ones, I searched for the rare and remarkable qualities inside each one? What new patterns, I began to wonder, would I find? Which ones would I identify with? Which ones would I strive to be?

Maybe, I said to myself, I could apply my new identification skills to those familiar trees and, with my new keys, finally go beyond mere facial recognition. I could even keep track of my observations, maybe learn the history of other neighborhoods, record my thoughts, collect their stories, and speak on their behalf in a field guide of my own.

Talk, said the Chinese scholar, does not cook rice.

THE PHILADELPHIA
UNDERSTORY
Table of Contents

COMING SOON

VOLUME TWO

MORE TALES FROM
THE PHILADELPHIA UNDERSTORY

I'd never seen anything like it before. It looked made out of spare parts, or made in someone's garage. There were long, thin gashes in the aluminum, like somebody had attacked it with a sword. How old was it? That was hard to tell but the sign looked very old.

Henry stepped up to the sign and ran his hand down the pole. "Where's it come from?" he asked.

"I don't know," I said, "but I think I know just the guy to ask."

Maybe it was the constant drizzle, maybe it was the holiday spirit, but eventually the scenery of the cemetery dampened my adventurous mood. An unsettling sense of the morbid and the macabre clouded my heart and rattled my walking bones.

The population of the cemetery was finally catching up to me.

COMING SOON

MORE TALES FROM
THE PHILADELPHIA UNDERSTORY

*This was the site of William Penn's most
legendary achievement, where he made his
great treaty with the Lenni-Lenape people.
Like most legendary achievements, it all
happened under a tall and mighty elm.*

DEEPER DIVES,
LONGER HIKES,
BIGGER MYSTERIES
IN THE
PHILLY
WILDS

"You better tighten up," he yelled into the phone. "And listen up too. This plan on yours can risk my job and whatever's left of your reputation. Worst case scenario and you put the whole city at risk. And for one tree? It's got zero chance. And with your latest string of bad luck that puts the chances at less than zero."

I yelled right back. "Never tell me the odds, Goldberg."

When it came to produce, by February, we're stuck with the kinds of vegetables that do well in storage but that take a bit of work in the kitchen: winter squash, potatoes, cabbage, turnips, rutabagas, beetroots, and certain kinds of radishes that nobody likes.

COMING SOON

MORE TALES FROM
THE PHILADELPHIA UNDERSTORY

"No spoilers," Gina said.

"Spoilers? I'll tell you the ending right now. Why not? It's already been told hundreds of times before. All the plants and animals of Turtle Island get together in a big circle and save the world."

"No way," I said but when I turned around there was Coyote in my kitchen with other plans for me in mind.

The moment he started whispering in my ear I knew I was doomed for the frying pan.

COMING SOON

VOLUME THREE

Made in the USA
Middletown, DE
09 December 2023